# Best Bush, Coast and Village Walks of South-East Tasmania

By
Ingrid Roberts

WOODSLANE

Woodslane Press Pty Ltd
10 Apollo St, Warriewood, NSW 2102
Email: info@woodslane.com.au
Website: www.travelandoutdoor.com.au

First printed in Australia in 2013 by Woodslane Press
© 2013 Woodslane Press, text © Ingrid Roberts

National Library of Australia Cataloguing-in-Publication entry

Author:          Roberts, Ingrid.

Title:           Best bush, coast and village walks of South East Tasmania /
                 Ingrid Roberts.

ISBN:            9781922131195 (pbk.)

Subjects:        Trails--Tasmania, Southeast--Guidebooks.
                 Nature trails--Tasmania, Southeast--Guidebooks.
                 Walking--Tasmania, Southeast--Guidebooks.
                 Tasmania, Southeast--Description and travel.
                 Tasmania, Southeast--Guidebooks.

Dewey Number:    796.5109946


Printed in China by Bookbuilders
Designed by Coral Lee
Main cover image by Ingrid Roberts

# Contents

Regional map.................................................................................. iv

Location maps ..........................................................................v-vii

Introduction ...................................................................................1

    Access to walks ...................................................................... 2

    Walk grades and times........................................................... 2

    What to take with you............................................................ 4

    Walking with children ............................................................ 5

    Taking your dog...................................................................... 5

    Looking after the environment ............................................. 6

    Bushwalking clubs.................................................................. 7

    Safety...................................................................................... 7

Walks at a glance......................................................................... 10

**Best Bush, Coast and Village Walks of South-East Tasmania**

    Freycinet National Park.........................................................15

    Maria Island.......................................................................... 40

    East Coast ............................................................................ 64

    Tasman Peninsula ................................................................ 98

    Midlands Villages ................................................................128

    Forest Reserves and Other Protected Areas ..................... 152

    Far South ..............................................................................178

Plant name glossary.................................................................. 216

Index .......................................................................................... 220

Further reading ..........................................................................224

About the author and acknowledgements.................................225

Other books from Woodslane ....................................................227

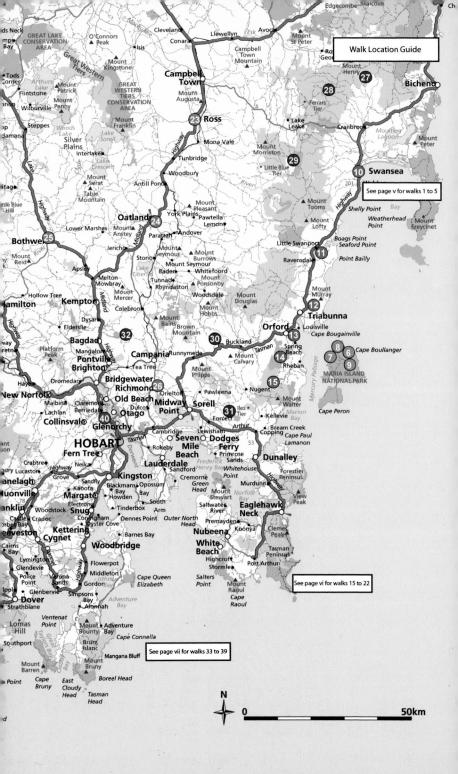

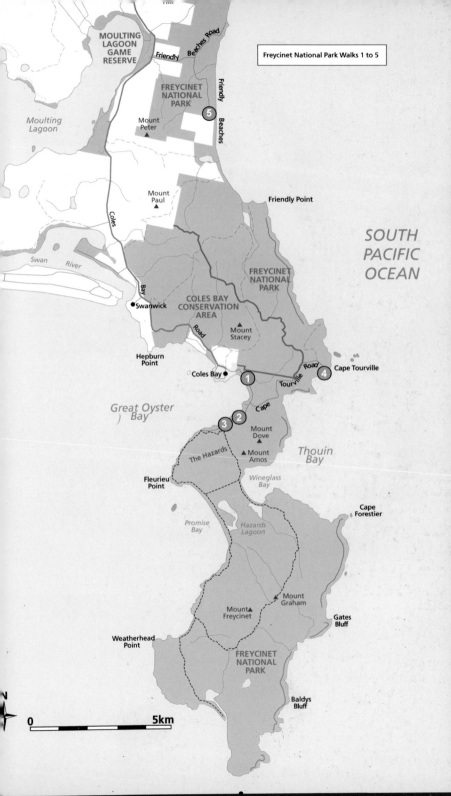

MOULTING
LAGOON
GAME
RESERVE

Friendly

Beaches Road

Freycinet National Park Walks 1 to 5

FREYCINET
NATIONAL
PARK

Moulting
Lagoon

Mount
Peter

Friendly

Beaches

⑤

Coles

Mount
Paul

Friendly Point

SOUTH
PACIFIC
OCEAN

Swan    River

Bay

Swanwick

FREYCINET
NATIONAL
PARK

COLES BAY
CONSERVATION
AREA

Mount
Stacey

Road

Hepburn
Point

Coles Bay

①

Road

Cape Tourville

④

Tourville

Cape

Great Oyster
Bay

③    ②

Mount
Dove

Thouin
Bay

▲ Mount
Amos

The Hazards

Wineglass
Bay

Fleurieu
Point

Cape
Forestier

Promise
Bay

Hazards
Lagoon

Mount▲
Freycinet

▲ Mount
Graham

Gates
Bluff

Weatherhead
Point

FREYCINET
NATIONAL
PARK

Baldys
Bluff

N

0    5km

v

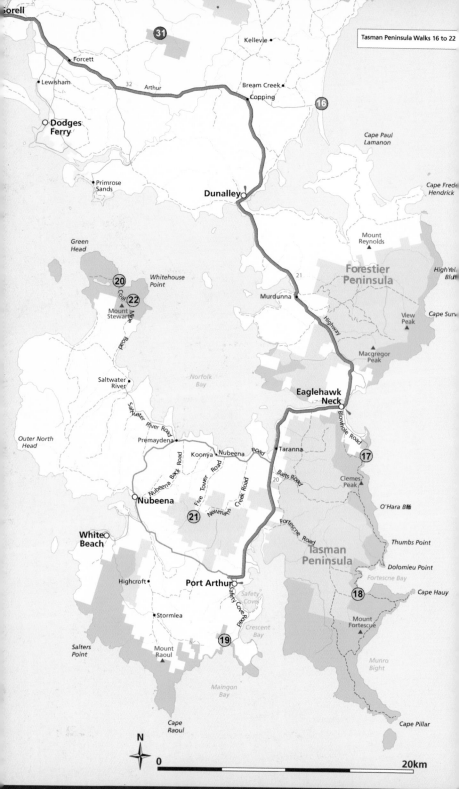

Tasman Peninsula Walks 16 to 22

Kellevie

Forcett

Lewisham

32   Arthur

Copping

Bream Creek

Cape Paul
Lamanon

Dodges
Ferry

Primrose
Sands

Dunalley

Cape Frede
Hendrick

Mount
Reynolds

Green
Head

Whitehouse
Point

Forestier
Peninsula

HighYel
Blu

Mount
Stewarts

Coal Mine Road

Murdunna

View
Peak

Cape Surv

Saltwater
River

Norfolk
Bay

Highway

Macgregor
Peak

Outer North
Head

Saltwater River Road

Premaydena

Koonya   Nubeena

Nubeena Road

Taranna

Eaglehawk
Neck

Blowhole Road

Clemes
Peak

O'Hara Blu

Nubeena Back Road

Five Tower Road

Newmans Creek Road

20

Balts Road

White
Beach

Nubeena

Highcroft

Stormlea

Salters
Point

Mount
Raoul

Port Arthur

Safety Cove Road

Safety
Cove

Crescent
Bay

Fortescue Road

Tasman
Peninsula

Thumbs Point

Dolomieu Point

Fortescue Bay

Cape Hauy

Mount
Fortescue

Munro
Bight

Cape Pillar

Maingon
Bay

Cape
Raoul

N

0                                    20km

Far South Walks 33 to 39

# Introduction

Tasmania's East Coast generally enjoys a milder climate than the more wind-battered West Coast. Rainfall is lower, temperatures are higher and seas are calmer. The walks in this book guide you to some much loved and often visited iconic features, as well as to some tranquil lesser known landmarks.

There are long, pristine beaches to enjoy and some of the island's unique fauna to meet. In spring and summer there will be an array of wildflowers to greet you as a bonus. There will be a chance to learn about Tasmania's convict past, early industries and farming practices.

The walks in this book explore the stunning scenery shaped by colourful granites that were intruded during the Devonian, including the smooth granite outcrops on Freycinet Peninsula, Maria Island, Tasman Peninsula

and the Hippolyte Rocks to the east of the Tasman Peninsula. Classic examples of Tasmania's signature rock, Jurassic dolerite, with its distinctive 'organ pipe' columns and up to 450-metre tall sea cliffs can be found on the Tasman Peninsula at Cape Hauy and the Snowy Range above Lake Skinner. You can be certain that the same places we enjoy today were also cherished by the Tasmanian Aborigines, whose knowledge of the land and its flora and fauna, passed down orally through

# Introduction

the generations, has unfortunately largely been discontinued through the thoughtless actions of many of the first white settlers. Spare a thought for the first Tasmanians as you tread in their ancient footsteps.

Walking is one of the best ways to really experience the natural environment. As a bonus it keeps you fit and allows you to drink in a daily dose of sunshine.

Where possible, circuit walks have been chosen in preference to return (there-and-back) walks. Don't be discouraged by return walks though, because you are likely to notice landscape features on your way back that you could not have seen on your way in, as you were facing in the opposite direction!

## Getting there

The *Walks at a glance* section at the beginning of each walk description contains information about how to reach the start of the walk by car. If you are travelling by bus you can check bus route numbers and obtain more detailed information from the Metro Hotline T 132201, visit the Metro shop next to the GPO in Hobart or go to www.metrotas.com.au online.

A number of companies run services to the start of popular walking tracks either on a regular basis or as a charter service. Contact the following for more information:

Evans Coaches T (03) 6297 1335

McDermotts Coaches T (03) 6394 3535

Maxwell's Coaches T (03) 6492 1431

Outdoor Recreational Transport T (03) 6391 8249

Tasmanian Wilderness Experiences T (03) 6261 4971

Tassie Link T 1300 300 520

Tiger Wilderness Bushwalkers Bus T 0428 308 813

## Walk grades

These are based on the Australian National Track Grading System which has standardised levels of difficulty ranging from Grades 1 to 5, where 1 is the easiest. Grade 1 tracks can be accessed by wheelchair and Grade

5 tracks are for very experienced bushwalkers only. The walks in this guide range from Grade 2, described in this guide as **Easy**, to Grades 3, described as **Medium** or 4, described as **Hard**.

**Easy** – Clearly marked tracks; some short steep gradients or sets of steps; few if any natural obstacles. Generally suitable for children unless stated otherwise, but see *Walking with children* for more details (supervision is essential in areas where there are unfenced cliff tops, busy roads to cross or next to watercourses).

**Medium** – Suitable for people of average fitness; marked tracks or routes, some of which may be overgrown. Longer steep gradients and natural obstacles such as fallen logs and rocks.

**Hard** – Suitable for experienced and fit walkers; marked tracks or routes sometimes rough or overgrown, or wet with steep gradients and natural obstacles such as rocks and fallen logs.

## Walking times

Each walk includes a grade, and the time necessary to complete it. These times are estimates only, and you may find that you are a lot faster or slower, depending on your age, fitness level, and whether you are a regular bushwalker. The times are based on a walking speed of 3km per hour, on flat ground, with allowances for gradients and longer walks. They are not designed to create a challenge and are just a base for you to work from — after completing one or two of these walks you will be able to judge how to adjust the walk times for yourself.

In the real world, walk times are affected by whether you are keen to stop and admire natural wonders that you encounter along the way, or take lots of photos, and whether you have curious toddlers or dogs in tow or just like to frequently stop for a rest and a snack or two. The larger the walking party the longer the walking time. Always err on the side of caution when estimating grades and times for yourself; it is better to have a little extra time on hand than to run into the dark or to miss arranged transport or important appointments.

# Introduction

Providing you are healthy (check this with your doctor if you are new to walking), you need not be discouraged by steep hills or longer climbs. Just remember we all puff when we go uphill; having to lift our own weight is not easy for anyone. Reduce your speed to allow your body to get used to the idea and plod on – you may surprise yourself how far you get! A good general rule is to start off with the easy, short walks and work up to the longer, harder ones. Poor weather conditions can make easy walks more hazardous by causing tracks to become slippery, for example.

## What to take with you

Wear non-cotton trousers (cotton is just awful when it gets wet) and carry a set of thermals, warm gloves, a beanie, a sun hat, a warm jacket and a raincoat in your backpack all year round. This will allow you to feel smug when the weather changes!

Your feet deserve to be looked after; they do a lot of work. For all of the walks in this book graded Easy/Medium you are advised to wear strong, comfortable walking shoes or trainers with a good grip that have been 'run in'. For the harder walks, half boots or boots are essential. Wear soft socks to prevent blisters and carry bandaids to cover blisters as soon as you notice them. Keep toenails trimmed.

It is wise to carry plenty of drinking water; on hot days at least one litre per person for every two hours of walking. A flask of hot water and separate tea, coffee, cocoa or soup powder (according to your taste) can also be a real lifesaver. Always carry some nibbles in the form of mixed nuts, dried fruit, seeds and chocolate or jelly beans for those moments when walking power fades, particularly with children, but also as emergency food. Carry both water and nibbles where they are readily accessible to prevent that 'Oh, I'll put off drinking because I can't be bothered to stop' scenario which will get you dehydrated in no time. For longer walks don't forget to take plenty of food.

Be aware that entry fees apply to all National Parks.

## Walking with children

While many of the walks in this guide are suitable for children, only a parent can judge what their child can manage. Some walks lead along unfenced cliff-tops and watercourses or require a road crossing, and parental supervision is essential. A ratio of one adult per child is ideal, but with older children you can probably get away with one adult to two children. Very young children are often more capable of walking than one would think: sometimes they complain of tiredness but really mean they are a bit overawed by the wide open spaces. Providing them with short-term goals such as reaching a nearby feature, giving them things to look for and periodically resting to hand out 'go food' will reassure them.

## Taking your dog

As a rule dogs are not allowed in National Parks, whereas reserves and other public spaces generally require you to walk dogs on a leash. Adhere to local signage. You will find that suitable walks for your four-legged friend are marked in the *Walks at a glance* section.

# Introduction

## Track closures

Tracks can be closed or rerouted for a variety of unforeseeable reasons such as flooding, bushfires, fallen trees or unstable ground. Closure can also be due to track developments and maintenance. For information on this, contact the relevant authority, either Parks and Wildlife Service T (03) 6233 6560 or www.parks.tas.gov.au, or the local council of the area.

## Looking after the environment

There seem to be a lot of rules about bushwalking, but when you analyse them you will see that most of them come under the common sense umbrella and are quite easy to make into a habit. They are there to help everyone to enjoy the wonderful experience of exploring new tracks in a 'cared-for environment'. So go out and enjoy!

Leaflets on minimal impact bushwalking are available from the Parks and Wildlife Service but in short the term means;

**Take your rubbish out with you**

**Stay on tracks**

**Don't pick wildflowers**

**Don't interfere with wildlife**

**Respect historical or cultural sites**

**Don't light fires** – Tasmanian plants, such as gum trees and the leaf litter beneath them, contain highly flammable oils that will ignite readily with just one spark, particularly on hot windy days in summer, and turn into a wildfire in minutes. If you are a smoker, please put out your cigarette butt very carefully indeed.

Please help to prevent the spread of the terrible root rot fungus *Phytophthora cinnamomi* by removing any soil (the carrier of this disease) from your gear, especially your boots, after every walk and when requested by signage.

The location of public toilets are indicated where available for each walk, but if you must go during a walk make sure you are well off the track (hang something brightly coloured on a tree to find your way back) and away from water courses. Use as little paper as possible. Bury waste to a depth of at least 10 cm – the aim is to reach the root zones of plants where it will act as compost. This is respectful both to the environment, and to the other walkers who will pass this way

## Bushwalking clubs

Tasmania has a number of bushwalking groups that cater for young and old. If you like walking in a larger group and want to tap into their vast amount of local knowledge, contact them and join the one that suits you best. Useful information about bushwalking and groups can be found at www.bushwalkingaustralia.org.au where Tasmanian Clubs are listed.

## Safety tips

For some of the longer walks, especially with children, it is wise to carry some basic first-aid gear such as a triangular bandage, an elastic bandage, bandaids, antiseptic cream, sachet of salt (to remove leeches), a small amount of vinegar or similar (to treat insect bites) and painkillers as well as some emergency gear such as a short candle, matches (for lighting a fire), whistle, pocket knife, safety pins, small torch, toilet paper and a foil rescue blanket (available in outdoor shops). Keep in a strong, see-through bag for easy access.

The risk of sunburn is high in Tasmania particularly during daylight saving time. Make sure you have sunscreen and wear a broad-brimmed hat from mid-morning to mid-afternoon to protect yourself.

A very old Tasmanian joke is "if you don't like the weather – come back in half an hour". Bear this in mind when you set off on a walk. Weather changes occur rapidly and often without warning, especially at higher

# Introduction

altitudes (snowfalls have been recorded on Mt Wellington, even in summer!).

Hypothermia is also a very real risk in Tasmania. Caused by prolonged exposure to cold, wet and windy conditions without adequate protection, hypothermia occurs when your body loses heat faster than it can produce it. Because it happens gradually and affects your thinking, you may not realise you need help, which makes it especially dangerous. Symptoms can include shivering, slurred speech, lethargy, stumbling, disturbed vision and irrational behaviour. Hypothermia can be prevented by being well prepared (see above).Treat by providing shelter, dry clothes and/or body heat from a fit companion. Give warm drinks and chocolate and send for help. Do not apply direct heat, massage or give alcohol.

### Jack jumper stings

Jack jumpers are very common in Tasmania. They build and live in crumbly looking mounds. They have a 1-centimetre long black body and orange pincers and legs. They jump at their victim and hold on with their pincers then sting with their tail, much like wasps. Jack jumpers can cause a severe allergic reaction, known as anaphylaxis, in susceptible people, which can be life threatening. Symptoms can include a rash, tightening of the throat, swelling of the lips and face and difficulty in breathing. Immediate medical treatment is needed. If you know you are allergic, consult your doctor who may prescribe adrenaline/EpiPen as an emergency medication to be carried.

### Snakes

The incidence of snake bite is very low in Tasmania and the incidence of death by snake bite is even lower. Although all three Tasmanian snake species are very venomous, they tend to slither off as soon as they feel the ground vibrate from your footsteps. If you do manage to surprise one in its favourite sunbaking spot, stand still until it retreats or give it a wide berth.

In the unlikely event that you do get bitten, stay calm and keep still to avoid speeding up your blood circulation. Place some padding over the bite and apply a firm bandage. If possible immobilise the affected limb by using a splint. Send someone for help or use your mobile phone if you are within range.

## Navigation

This guide book or a photocopy of the relevant walk pages will hopefully give you sufficient descriptions to keep you on track and out of trouble. When following a route with cairns or markers make sure you can see the next one before proceeding, especially in foggy conditions. Some of the walks in this book describe tracks that are indistinct in places and for this reason you are advised to carry a regional map and compass (and know how to use them), particularly for walks in more remote areas.

If you suspect that you are lost, stay on tracks where you will be easier to locate by anyone looking for you. Try and call for help, 000 or 112 (the international emergency number for mobile phones only). Even if your mobile doesn't have enough signal strength to make a call, try sending an SMS to someone trustworthy, as this will have a better chance of getting through (at the time of writing, it is not possible to send an SMS to 000 or 112). Give as clear an indication as you can of your position; describe the landscape around you, whether you are on a ridge or in a valley, whether there is water nearby and where the sun is in the sky. Make yourself visible by spreading out anything brightly coloured on the ground or, if possible, lighting an emergency fire with lots of smoke.

EPIRBs and satellite phones can be hired from Parks and Wildlife Service.

Walk with at least one companion and let someone know where you are going and when you expect to return.

# Walks at a glance

| No | Walk | Distance | Time |
|----|------|----------|------|
| **Freycinet National Park** | | | |
| 1 | Coles Bay Circuit | 6.5 circuit | 3 hrs |
| 2 | Wineglass Bay to Hazards Beach Circuit | 11 circuit | 4 hrs 30 mins |
| 3 | Mount Amos | 3.5 return | 4 hrs |
| 4 | Sleepy Bay to Bluestone Bay | 7 return | 2 hrs |
| 5 | Exploring Friendly Beaches | 12 return | 3 hrs 30 mins |
| **Maria Island** | | | |
| 6 | Bishop and Clerk | 9 return | 4 hrs 30 mins |
| 7 | Oast House and Painted Cliffs Circuit | 5.1 circuit | 2 hrs |
| 8 | Quarries and Fossil Cliffs Circuit | 5.5 circuit | 2 hrs 30 mins |
| 9 | Convict Reservoir Circuit | 6 circuit | 2 hrs |
| **East Coast** | | | |
| 10 | Swansea Seaside Village | 4.8 circuit | 1 hrs 30 mins |
| 11 | Lisdillon Saltworks and Beach | 5.5 circuit | 2 hrs |
| 12 | Triabunna | 4.4 circuit | 1 hr 30 mins |
| 13 | Shelly Beach to Spring Beach | 6.4 return | 1 hr 45 mins |
| 14 | The Three Thumbs | 4.5 circuit | 2 hrs 30 mins |
| 15 | Wielangta Walk | 5.7 return | 3 hrs |
| 16 | The Long Spit to Marion Bay | 6.6 circuit | 2 hrs |
| **Tasman Peninsula** | | | |
| 17 | Devils Kitchen to Waterfall Bluff | 6.75 return | 3 hrs 15 min |
| 18 | Cape Hauy | 10.5 return | 5 hrs |
| 19 | Crescent Bay and Mount Brown | 9.5 return | 4 hrs 30 mins |
| 20 | Lime Bay, Lagoon Beach and Green Head Circuit | 8.5 circuit | 3 hrs 30 mins |
| 21 | Clark Cliffs | 7.4 return | 3 hrs |
| 22 | Mount Stewart - Coal Mines Circuit | 6.7 circuit | 2 hrs 15 mins |

| Grade | Public Transport | Café | Dogs | Highlights |
|---|---|---|---|---|
| easy | yes | yes | no | beach, views, granite outcrops, park |
| medium/hard | yes | no | no | lookouts, beaches, bays, bushland |
| hard | yes | no | no | panoramic views, granite |
| easy/medium | no | no | no | lookout, coastal cliffs, bushland |
| easy | no | no | no | beach, lagoons, birdlife |
| medium/hard | yes | no | no | seacliffs, mountain views, wildlife |
| easy | yes | no | no | history, bushland, beach, sandstone cliffs |
| medium | yes | no | no | history, seacliffs, water views, wildlife |
| easy | yes | no | no | history, bush, reservoir, wildlife |
| easy | yes | yes | yes | history, beach, waterviews |
| easy | no | no | no | history, beach, waterviews |
| easy | yes | yes | yes | harbour, wildlife, history |
| easy | no | no | yes* | beaches, seacliffs, wildflowers, history |
| easy/medium | no | no | yes | bush, flora, views |
| easy/medium | no | no | yes | bush, tall trees, river, history |
| easy | no | no | no | beach, dunes, birdlife |
| medium | yes | no | no | seacliffs, erosion features, ocean views, waterfall |
| medium | yes | no | no | seacliffs, erosion features, ocean views |
| medium | no | no | no | flora, panoramic views, beach |
| easy | no | no | no | bush, beach, ocean views, sandstone cliffs |
| medium | no | no | yes | tall trees, musk forest, birdlife, cliffs |
| easy | no | no | no | history, bush, views, birdlife |

# Walks at a glance

| No | Walk | Distance | Time |
|----|------|----------|------|
| **Midlands Villages** | | | |
| 23 | Ross | 4.4 circuit | 1 hr 30 mins |
| 24 | Oatlands Historic Village | 4.3 circuit | 1 hr 15 mins |
| 25 | Bothwell Higland Village | 2.1 circuit | 1 hr |
| 26 | Historic Richmond | 2.5 circuit | 1 hr |
| **Forest Reserves and Other Protected Areas** | | | |
| 27 | Hardings Falls | 1.2 circuit | 1 hr |
| 28 | Meetus Falls | 1 return | 45 mins |
| 29 | Lost Falls and Scenic Lookout | 1.3 return | 45 mins |
| 30 | Tasmanian Bushland Garden | 1.4 circuit | 1 hr |
| 31 | Woodvine Reserve | 5 return | 1 hrs 30 mins |
| 32 | Chauncy Vale to Flat Rock Lookout | 11 return | 5 hrs |
| **Far South** | | | |
| 33 | Mount Misery | 6.2 return | 3 hrs 30 mins |
| 34 | Billy Browns Falls | 8 return | 5 hrs |
| 35 | Lake Skinner | 8.8 return | 5 hrs 30 mins |
| 36 | Garden Island Bay Coastal Walk | 4.5 return | 1 hr 45 mins |
| 37 | Duckhole Lake | 4.3 return | 1 hr 30 mins |
| 38 | Southport Lagoon | 6.6 circuit | 2 hrs |
| 39 | Fishers Point | 7 return | 2 hrs 15 mins |
| 40 | Montrose to MONA | 8.2 return | 3 hrs (+ museum visit) |

*Dogs must be kept on leash

| Grade | Public Transport | Café | Dogs | Highlights |
|---|---|---|---|---|
| easy | yes | yes | yes | history, bridge, river, farmland |
| easy | yes | yes | yes* | history, lake, flour mill |
| easy | yes | yes | yes | history, river, farmland, forest |
| easy | yes | yes | yes | history, bridge, river, arts and crafts |
| medium | no | no | yes* | forest, waterfall |
| easy | no | no | yes* | forest, waterfall |
| easy | no | no | yes* | waterfall, forest, lookout |
| easy | no | no | no | gardens, bushland, creek, views |
| easy | no | no | no | farming history, bushland, flora, views |
| medium | no | no | no | bushland, tall trees, flora, creek, views |
| medium | no | no | no | tall trees, views, sandstone cliff, fern gully |
| hard | no | no | yes | tall trees, birdlife, views, waterfall |
| hard | no | no | no | bushland, flora, mountain views, lake |
| easy | yes | no | no | bushland, flora, sandstone cliffs, coastal views, beaches |
| easy | no | no | yes | bushland, creek, sinkhole lake |
| easy | yes | yes | no | history, railway, bushland, beach |
| easy | no | no | no | history, beach, views |
| medium | yes | yes | yes | parkland, playground, museum, waterviews |

# Freycinet National Park

Freycinet National Park together with Cradle Mountain-Lake St Clair National Park is one of the most visited natural attractions in Tasmania. This is not surprising, as the scenery is absolutely superb. Its value was officially recognised in the early 1900s when the area was first made into a reserve. The park largely comprises a peninsula of some thirty kilometres length from north to south. It is attached to Tasmania's east coast, with Great Oyster Bay separating it from mainland Tasmania. The Freycinet Peninsula was named after the brothers Freycinet of the French scientific expedition led by Baudin in 1802.

The most visible and awe-inspiring feature of the park is The Hazards: a spectacular range of five pink and red granite mountains which have a north-east to south-west orientation just south of Coles Bay. These magnificent mountains overlook beautiful Wineglass Bay which is nestled below them to the south. The following chapter invites you on a stroll around the little township of Coles Bay – the commercial centre of the Freycinet Peninsula – and longer walks to some famous locations and some lesser known treasures within the park.

# 1 Coles Bay Circuit

The coastal walk described below allows uninterrupted views of The Hazards – they are particularly spectacular during late afternoon and evening when lit by the sun. The little township of Coles Bay originally attracted whalers, who operated from Wineglass Bay, Shouten Island (to the south) and The Fisheries (near the start of the main walking tracks) for a short period beginning in the 1820s. In the early 1900s people began to build holiday shacks around the area. An upmarket holiday chateau was built by Ronald Richardson, a former bank clerk, in 1934 at the northern end of Richardsons Beach. The chateau underwent redevelopment in the 1990s, becoming the present-day Freycinet Lodge.

## At a glance

**Grade:** Easy

**Time:** 3 hrs

**Distance:** 6.5 km circuit

**Ascent/Descent:** 20 m/20 m

**Conditions:** Mix of beach, footpaths and optional coastal rock-hopping, some street crossings

**Further information:** www.parks.tas.gov.au

### Getting there

**Car:** Take Tasman Highway (A3) and turn into Coles Bay Road 11 kilometres south of Bicheno. After 27 kilometres pass the turnoff into Coles Bay township and continue past the Parks Visitor Centre to a small car park signed *Richardsons Beach Southern Day Use Area* just before Freycinet Lodge

The Hazards from Coles Bay

## Walk directions

**1** Walk down to Richardsons Beach and turn right to walk to its far end. This beach is well visited, particularly during the warmer summer months when you can see happy campers from the extensive camping areas behind the beach enjoying the calm, clear, turquoise waters of Coles Bay. You will also note that kayaking and boating are popular with locals and visitors alike. The grand views across to The Hazards from here are truly world-class.

**2** Cross a small granite outcrop to a shorter section of Richardsons Beach and walk its length as well.

**3** Go right at a wooden *Track to Shop* sign, then keep left at a junction. The track leads up along the contour of the headland that the small town perches on. The bush here is dominated by she-oaks and prickly box. You will pass a National Parks boundary sign before the track emerges at the end of Esplanade East.

**4** Here you have the option of taking a narrow steep bush track about 12 metres from the end of the esplanade which leads back down to the rocky shore for a fun stretch of rock-hopping along the shore. Alternatively you can take the 'high road' and continue along the esplanade, which is the preferred option at high tide or in wet conditions. Going along the rocky shore you will soon pass some boat sheds and a public jetty.

**5** Turn right into Garnet Street and continue on to Jetty Road, which is also the main access road to Coles Bay township.

**6** Go left down Jetty Road until you reach the jetty for Wineglass Bay Cruises.

**7** Carefully cross the jetty access towards the Esplanade. This leads along the south-western boundary of Coles

# 1 Coles Bay Circuit

Bay along a particularly spectacular stretch of coastline which you can access from the Esplanade via a number of rough side tracks (the first one starts just past the power pole on the western side of the jetty). Most of these paths lead onto pink and red granite shelves and boulders encrusted in the bright orange lichen which you see so often along the east coast of Tasmania. People love to engage in a spot of fishing along here or just sit and enjoy the scenery.

**8** You will pass a car park and picnic area adjacent to a particularly beautiful granite outcrop which juts into the sea.

**9** After about one kilometre you will reach Muirs Beach with its small park and picnic area. Opposite the esplanade are a supermarket, service station and a number of eateries catering for all comers as well as an adjoining holiday centre's transient population. This is about halfway along your circuit and perhaps a good place to rest and enjoy some food.

**10** To continue, return along the Esplanade to Harold Street and go left, then left again into Brooker Street which after a short while degenerates into a rough vehicle track lined

with bull oaks, Oyster Bay pines, native cherries and kunzeas. The gritty sand beneath your feet is obviously granitic.

**11** The track emerges in Cosgrove Street. Turn left and go down to

a right-hand corner where the road changes its name to Percy Street.

**12** At the corner a sign points to a nearby lookout which you can visit if so inclined. It consists of a low wooden structure which can be climbed to view the tops of trees which have obviously grown since it was built. Otherwise continue along Percy Street until you reach its junction with Jetty Road.

**13** Go right, walk back down to Garnet Street and then retrace your steps to the start.

## Tasmanian history – Early occupation of Coles Bay

For thousands of years the Toorernomairremener people, a band of about 50 family members who belonged to the about 600- to 700-strong Oyster Bay tribe called this area home during winter when they would seek seafood, warmth and shelter from the harsher climate in their midlands hunting grounds. Their middens (refuse dumps of heritage and scientific value) have been found along Richardsons Beach and on Hazards Beach. The type of food they ate is recorded in layers of the middens. It seems they largely feasted on oysters (not sustainable today!) and other shellfish.

Silas Coles was one of the early white settlers of Coles Bay and gave the area its name. Unfortunately he was an enterprising man and burnt large amounts of shells from the abovementioned middens in the 1830s for the purpose of lime production. The lime was shipped to nearby Swansea to be used in mortar. Today, good old Silas would have incurred a hefty fine for disturbing an Aboriginal site.

Richardsons Bay

## Out and about – Australian Three Peaks Race

Coles Bay is one of the three locations for the Australian Three Peaks Race, a running and sailing event which begins near Launceston and ends in Hobart. Runners speed up and down the tallest peak on the peninsula, the 620-metre high Mount Freycinet, in a gruelling 33-kilometre leg of this race which takes place at Easter time. Mount Freycinet can be seen to the right of Mount Graham looking south from the Wineglass Bay Lookout and from the summit of Mount Amos (see Walks 2 and 3).

# 2 Wineglass Bay to Hazards Beach Circuit

The most visited area in the Freycinet National Park is a lookout in The Hazards, in a saddle between Mount Amos and Mount Mayson. From here visitors can view the perfectly shaped Wineglass Bay and its crystal clear waters. This iconic track, which forms part of your circuit walk, is very much designed with walkers in mind, but manages to remain aesthetically pleasing and sympathetic to the natural environment. The imaginative use of local granite to incorporate natural features such as trees and boulders into the hard landscape design, which includes dry stone retaining walls, paving and sets of 'stairs', makes for an interesting and easy ascent. The descent into Wineglass Bay is less landscaped — with correspondingly less traffic — while the rest of the circuit consists of a beautifully relaxing walk through natural bushland with interesting understorey plants. Two lovely beaches, Wineglass Bay Beach and Hazards Beach add extra variety to this must-do walk.

Granite Tors on Mt Mason

## At a glance

**Grade:** Medium/Hard

**Time:** 4 hrs 30 mins + extra 50 mins return along Wineglass Bay beach

**Distance:** 11 km circuit + extra for a walk along Wineglass Bay as far as you like

**Ascent/Descent:** 180 m/180 m

**Conditions:** Mix of wide, well-built track and rocky and sandy bush tracks, mostly sheltered, parks passes apply

**Further information**: www.parks.tas.gov.au

### Getting there

**Car:** Take Tasman Highway (A3) and turn into Coles Bay Road 11 kilometres south of Bicheno. Drive to the end of the road (about 4 kilometres past the Visitor Centre) and park in the large designated walking track car park. Follow signage to start of walks and walker registration

## Walk directions

**1** Pass the walker registration and follow the wide, gravelled track signed *Wineglass Bay Lookout and Hazards Circuit,* ignoring the track to the left which leads to the summit of Mount Amos. The bush here is dominated by bull oaks, tea-tree and banksia with some eucalypts in the canopy. Very shortly the track splits around a beautiful silver peppermint feature tree and seat with views up to Mount Amos and to the valley formed by Fisheries Creek below.

**2** The track continues to Hazards Junction (where your return track from Hazards Beach joins on the right) and begins to climb and wind gently through dry bushland. As you cross another small watercourse you may be able to spot some interesting shrubs beside the track, including fringe myrtle with their pinkish flowers and long prominent stamens, yellow hakea, and *Leptospermum grandiflorum* or literally tea-tree with 'grand flowers'. Next you will reach an open lookout area with granite boulder seating.

**3** A stone staircase beside a large, long boulder allows you to gain some height, then

Wineglass Bay Lookout

the wide track lined with beautiful stone walling and the occasional handrail continues to snake uphill. The view to the river valley below becomes wider as you climb. You will pass a particularly large and long granite boulder from which water drips after rain. The track here is furnished with crazy paving as it leads through a narrow gap between two huge boulders. Shortly you can enjoy views from a lookout across Coles Bay and beyond to Moulting Lagoon.

**4** About twenty minutes from the start you come to *Boulderfield Junction* with the return track for visitors who wish to go back to the car park after having been to the Wineglass Bay Lookout. Another well-placed seat here invites you to rest before the final assault via many stone stairs to the saddle.

**5** At the saddle you will find an interesting wooden sculpture, the 'saddle seat', which was

constructed in the year 2000 by students from the Tasmanian School of Art. Just past this feature a short side track on the left leads to the well-visited lookout which is perched on top of huge boulders. From here you can, weather permitting, see across Wineglass Bay with Cape Forestier on your left, the tall mountain sitting above the bay is Mount Graham with the taller Mount Freycinet to its right.

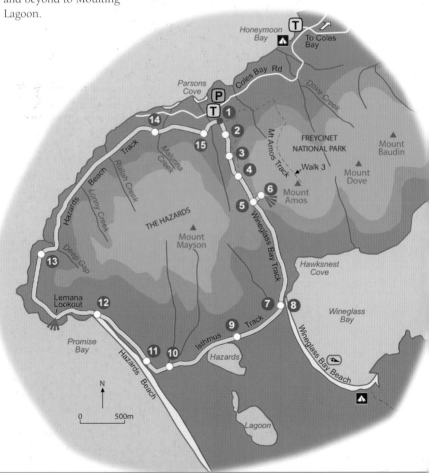

Saddle seat

**6** Enjoy the view then return to the main track to continue your walk. As the largest number of visitors return to the start from here, the track, now carrying much less traffic, becomes narrow and rocky. It leads down a steep, south-facing, shady gully forested with tall blue gums, Tasmanian blanket bush and saggs, towards Wineglass Bay and the beach. Some grass trees can also be found here. The track curves right and contours around huge granite buttresses. The thick vegetation which includes woolly tea-tree, prickly box and she-oak supports a rich variety of birdlife.

**7** After about 25 minutes the bush becomes more open as the track levels. You will note that some of the large blue gums have had their bases hollowed out by fire in the past. You will reach some interpretation panels (about the shorebirds to be found along the beach) at the turn-off to Hazards Beach. Return to this junction after you have enjoyed a small foray along Wineglass Bay Beach, which is well worth the effort.

**8** From the junction take the Hazards Beach via Isthmus Track which crosses a small creek that flows into the bay. The track runs north of Hazards Lagoon which lies between Wineglass Bay and Hazards Beach. This is a very relaxing section of your walk with occasional views across the lagoon on your left towards Mount Graham and Mount Freycinet.

**9** The track is sandy and level and can be a bit muddy after rain. It leads through lovely bushland with tall gums overhead as it curves around the base of Mount Mayson on the right. In the understorey you may, at different times of the year, find botanical delights such as the yellow, clustered pea flowers of the native daphne, the dainty white sprays of heath myrtle (which in Tasmania can only be found in the Bicheno to Coles Bay area), white kunzea and guitar plant, as well as a host of epacrids. The rich plant life of course attracts birds and you are likely to hear and see many of them, such as fantails, robins, thornbills and wattlebirds.

**10** Soon after crossing a swampy area on

## 2 Wineglass Bay to Hazards Beach Circuit

duckboarding and passing a small lagoon on the right, you will crest a large dune and emerge to overlook Hazards Beach with great views into Promise Bay with Promise Rock and Refuge Island. This area was occupied by the Oyster Bay tribe and many middens can be found along the edges of dunes.

**11** Go right and wander to the far end of Hazards Beach at the foot of Mount Mayson which you can see up ahead.

**12** Cross a small creek and then follow it and up into the she-oak forest where the track curves left to follow the rocky coast. You will pass a couple of photogenic coves with granite boulders and tiny beaches. Black peppermints grow in this dry forest. The track becomes rocky and is

Hazards Beach

crisscrossed with tree roots, which can be a real tripping hazard or send you off into a slide in wet weather.

**13** The track takes on a slight yo-yo effect as you cross some six creeks or watercourses that originate from the catchment area at the top of Mount Mayson. Each of these ups and downs has a slightly different character and you are rewarded with many fine views both out to the coast and inland to the spectacular granite tors above.

**14** Eventually you will note that the track leads further inland through woodland dominated by black peppermints then an open area with heath plants and a few lonely grass trees, with the explanation for their loneliness on a panel a little further along the track.

**15** Some long wooden steps lead down to the last creek crossing via some carefully placed stones and up some rocky stairs before the track becomes gravelly, widens and finally joins the Wineglass Bay Lookout track. Turn left to retrace your steps to the car park from here.

Wineglass Bay

## Tasmanian history – The Hazards

The Hazards mountain range is not named for being hazardous as one would expect! It was named after the Hazard family who ran a whaling operation in this area from 1824. The story goes that Captain Albert 'Black' Hazard's whaling boat 'Promise' was wrecked in Promise Bay. His crew awaited rescue on Refuge Island while the captain swam ashore, arduously walked around the base of Mount Mayson (before the lovely track you can walk now was built) and reached help at the hut of Silas Coles (an early settler who burnt shells for lime which was shipped to Swansea). The other small island in the bay is Promise Rock.

# 3 Mount Amos

This beautiful mountain was named for the early settlers Adam and John Amos. Margaret Amos became the first white woman to climb it. For an exhilarating birds-eye view down to the iconic Wineglass Bay and a moderately challenging rock climb this is the best walk on the peninsula. Natural rock sculptures made from granite abound along the way, and during spring and summer patches of wildflowers are an absolute delight.

Wineglass Bay from Mt Amos summit

## At a glance

**Grade:** Hard

**Time:** 4 hrs

**Distance:** 3.5 km return

**Ascent/Descent:** 414 m/414 m

**Conditions:** Steep climbing route on smooth granite, extremely slippery when moist or wet, exposed at higher altitude; well marked with coloured arrows painted on the granite, but you need to make sure you pay attention because it is easy to lose them

**Further information:**
www.parks.tas.gov.au

**Getting there**

**Car:** Take Tasman Highway (A3) and turn into Coles Bay Road 11 kilometres south of Bicheno. Drive to the end of the road (about 4 kilometres past the Visitor Centre) and park in the large designated walking track car park. Follow signage to start of walks and walker registration

## Walk directions

**1** Pass the walker registration and take the first track to the left, signed Mount Amos. A few steps further go left again passing a small reservoir. Banksias, bull oaks and tea-tree grow here with an understorey of sedges. Some duckboarding takes you across a small watercourse where you can see button grass and coral fern – two plant species that love wet spots.

**2** From here the track begins to climb via some rough stone steps and past most impressive granite boulders. Before long, as the track curves to the right, you gain views along Richardsons Beach across to Coles Bay and

Muirs Beach beyond. The bush here still bears the scars from a devastating fire that occurred more than 30 years ago.

**3** A warning sign appears before you step onto the first granite shelf. It would be wise to reassess the weather situation here and turn back if it looks inclement. Otherwise go straight ahead here. Climbing onto the bedrock you will note the first of the (left pointing) painted arrows that direct you along the route. Take care not to get your soles wet when

traversing seepage points to reduce the slipping hazard on the smooth granite.

**4** After passing a huge boulder and a round rock balanced on a plinth, head for an obvious gap between the two peaks that form the summit of Mount Amos.

**5** During the ascent you will scale several of the steep, bull-nosed ledges that are clearly visible from below. The last one is particularly steep and you will need both hands to practice your three-point climbing technique (making sure you have a firm hold on three of your points while moving the fourth – hand or foot!).

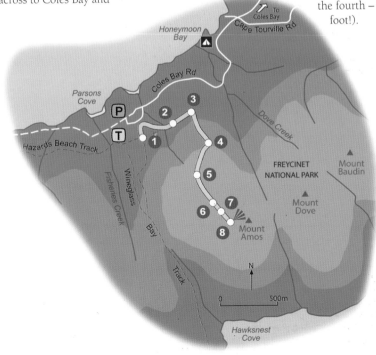

## 3 Mount Amos

**6** You then sidle along the right side of the left-hand (western), lower peak, through gigantic tors, a patch of bushland with stunted eucalypts and a small area of button grass.

**7** Next you will be heading for the eastern highest point and as you top the last granite boulder you will experience a sense of awe when you suddenly see the jewel in Tasmania's crown, Wineglass Bay, making the climb well worth its while. Indeed the view to the south is truly panoramic as the southern half of Freycinet Peninsula is laid out like a map beneath your feet. To the left is Cape Forestier with Lemon Rock attached to its end.

Let your eyes wander right along the sea cliffs towards Wineglass Bay Beach, the wetlands around Hazards Lagoons and Hazards Beach, with Mount Graham and Mount Freycinet towering above. On the horizon you can probably just make out Shouten Island which lies south of the peninsula.

Coles Bay from Mt Amos Track

## Tasmanian environment – Granite

The granite you see on Mount Amos and the Tasmanian East Coast in general is very old and dates back to Devonian times, which saw large intrusions of magma into the even older folded rock that went before. As the intruded

magma cooled very slowly, there was enough time to allow large crystals to grow, giving this granite its coarse-grained look. The rock above the intrusion has now worn away, having had about 350 million (give or take a few tens of millions) years to do so.

Red granite was quarried near The Fisheries by two Italian brothers from the early 1930s to 1997. Although the quarry operated for a long time, it was never very profitable. The granite was used for monuments, headstones and in buildings. The Hazards Beach track once led through the old quarry site but was later re-routed to join the Wineglass Bay track further south.

**8** Having enjoyed the scenery, it will be time to begin your downwards journey to the start point. You can allow yourself to feel satisfied about having 'bagged' this special Tasmanian peak!

Granite Ledges on Mt Amos

## Tasmanian environment – Button grass
### (*Gymnoschoenus sphaerocephalus*)

This member of the sedge family is the most common vegetation type in high

altitude and high rainfall areas, particularly in the west and south-west of Tasmania. In south-eastern Tasmania it can be found along creeks and in hollows, such as the one you will pass on the way up to the summit of Mount Amos. Button grass is able to thrive in very poor soils, where other plants struggle. Button grass moorlands are also highly adapted to fire. An amazingly large area of Tasmania, roughly one seventh, is covered in button grass.

# 4 Sleepy Bay to Bluestone Bay

This is a beautiful short walk within Freycinet National Park that explores Cape Tourville, Little Bluestone and Bluestone Bay, along with a walk variation that leads to the neighbouring Sleepy Bay. This walk, along with its walk variation, can easily be combined into a day's outing. On the eastern side of the peninsula, Cape Tourville and its lighthouse provide stunning end-on views of The Hazards with Mount Graham, Mount Freycinet and Cape Forestier in the background, as well as views eastwards out to the Tasman Sea to a clutch of little rocky islands, just off the coast, known as The Nuggets.

Little Bluestone

## At a glance

**Grade:** Easy/Medium

**Time:** 1 hr 45 mins (or 2 hours including walk variation)

**Distance:** 7 km return

**Ascent/Descent:** 60 m/60 m

**Conditions:** Mix of landscaped paths and rocky or sandy bush tracks, mostly sheltered, parks passes apply

**Further information:** www.parks.tas.gov.au

### Getting there

**Car:** Take the Tasman Highway (A3) and turn into Coles Bay Road, 11 kilometres south of Bicheno. 3 kilometres south of Coles Bay turn left into Cape Tourville Road. Continue 5 km to Cape Tourville car park. If exploring the walk variation, follow Cape Tourville Road for 1.5 kilometres from the turn into Coles Bay Road, and stop at the Sleepy Bay car park

## Walk directions

**1** From Cape Tourville car park, take the well-signposted and interpreted circuit walk to the right around the lighthouse. A section of the walk consists of an elaborate, fully fenced boardwalk that hugs the granite outcrop beneath. Near the lookout, markings on the boards under your feet indicate the actual lengths of seals, tuna, dolphins and various whales. A number of interpretive panels inform you about the history, birdlife and flora of the area. Finally you complete the circuit, along a winding path through pleasantly landscaped native flora.

**2** Head down Cape Tourville Road for about 200 metres to a small gravel parking bay by a *40 km limit* sign. Carefully cross the road and enter the 4WD track which after a few metres is signed *Bluestone Bay 2.3 km 4WD access*. Although traffic is usually very sparse you need to be aware that you are potentially sharing the track with vehicles.

**3** The road leads through dry bushland with a canopy of tall black peppermints and she-oaks, an understorey of banksias and tea-tree, and a groundcover of saggs. The road curves right and goes downhill for a short stretch, levels off then climbs slightly. You will note a change in vegetation with blue gums overhead, wattles and bracken fern and a patch of young grass trees. Nectar and insect-feeding birds can be seen going about their business in this pleasant bush environment.

**4** Turn right at a junction, pass a sign about keeping to formed roads and shortly the ocean will come into view. The track dips down slightly.

**5** After about ten minutes you will reach a road on your left signed *Bluestone Bay 300 m*. Continue straight ahead towards the Whitewater camp site for a small side trip of about half

Bluestone
Bay

Little Bluestone
Bay

The Nuggets

FREYCINET
NATIONAL
PARK

Cape Tourville Rd

CAPE
TOURVILLE

Carp
Bay

Sleepy
Bay

To Coles
Bay

N

0    500m

an hour to Little Bluestone. (Alternatively, skip ahead to waypoint 9 to continue straight to Bluestone Bay from here.)

**6** Before you reach the actual camp site turn right at a blue sign marked *Site closed for revegetation*, which applies to former more extensive camping areas along this track. There is a particularly large number of wattlebirds in this area and you may also hear the noisy butcherbirds and kookaburras.

**7** Keep right at an apparent Y-junction and follow the track which sidles downhill into a small gully. Take care with some tree roots that grow across the track. As you descend, the gully narrows and you will note a creek headed for Little Bluestone. Negotiate a few logs that have fallen across the track..

**8** Shortly you will emerge at the little bay and a careful, very short scramble will take you down to the rocky

foreshore. You can spend pleasant moments here observing shore birds or exploring the sculptural granite boulders. Looking east you can see the rocky Nuggets jutting out of the ocean, and across the bay some sheer cliffs which occasionally provide rock climbers with their thrills.

**9** Retrace your steps to the *Bluestone Bay 300 m* sign and descend through a she-oak forest.

**10** You soon arrive at Bluestone Bay, with its vivid turquoise waters. As the name implies, the 'beach' here consists of granite boulders worn into large, smooth egg shapes by the constant action of ocean waves. You will also find stands of native hop bushes. When you have enjoyed the scenery and perhaps had a bite to eat, retrace your steps to the start point.

The Nuggets

## Walk variation

A delightful walk variation starts at Sleepy Bay car park, 3.5 kilometres before Cape Tourville. From the sign at the start of the track, follow the track as it leads downhill and then curves right. There are a couple of unfenced lookouts along the way, so take care if you are walking with children.

You will be able to see Mount Parsons, the easternmost mountain of The Hazards range, and in the distance Mount Freycinet, Mount Graham and Cape Forestier. Continue to the small beach at the mouth of a creek that flows into the bay from the top of The Hazards. Its coarse sand has weathered from the granite above. Some beautifully sculptured pink granite boulders add interest and are photogenic. Early morning light is particularly lovely here.

## Tasmanian environment – 'Bluestone'

The colloquial name 'bluestone' is generally used for Tasmania's signature rock, the igneous dolerite. However the rocks at Bluestone Bay are a form of granite, probably better described as diorite, because although they are coarse-grained and have a high proportion of feldspars like the surrounding granites, they contain some dark minerals like hornblende which give them their distinctive blue colour.

Bluestone Bay

# 5 Exploring Friendly Beaches

Long beaches, a vast expanse of ever-changing dune fields (where even marker posts disappear in the shifting sands) and numerous lagoons are just waiting to be explored during this walk. The area is home to large numbers of shore birds and you will need to be mindful of their presence and take care not to disturb them or their nests. The birds do not appear to be overly shy however, and seem to be accustomed to the odd visit by a, hopefully friendly, humanoid. At the southern end of the walk lies Friendly Point made of granite. This is a wonderful resting and lookout spot. Although the walk can be undertaken any time, it is at its best during low tide when interesting rocks become exposed along the beach.

## At a glance

**Grade:** Easy
**Time:** 3 hrs 30 mins
**Distance:** 12 km return
**Conditions:** Sunny and exposed, sandy
**Further information:** www.parks.tas.gov.au

### Getting there

**Car:** Take Tasman Highway (A3) and turn into Coles Bay Road 11 kilometres south of Bicheno. After 8.5 kilometres turn left into Friendly Beaches Road. Drive past a registration booth and at 1.9 kilometres turn right onto an unmarked gravel road. Continue on for 2.4 kilometres and park in a small car park on left side of road

Friendly Beaches

# 5 Exploring Friendly Beaches

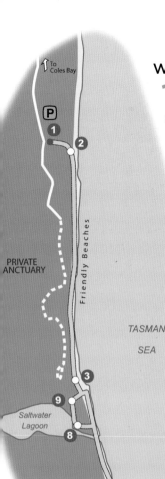

## Walk directions

**1** The narrow, sandy footpath begins at the northern end of the car park and heads eastward towards the coast through some dense coastal vegetation of manuka, banksia and boobyalla. The track is a bit braided but basically you are just heading for the coast where you will emerge in a few minutes. It is a good idea to make a note of your exit point for your return.

**2** Turn right when you reach the beach and begin walking along it towards the headland you can see in the distance.

**3** About halfway along this stretch of coastline the large Saltwater Lagoon comes into view. A detour along its eastern shore is planned for your return walk. Pass the lagoon for now and continue along the beach which becomes much wider here. You may be able to spot hooded plovers, pied oystercatchers and pacific gulls here as you near the rocky headland of Friendly Point.

**4** You will pass Freshwater Lagoon just before the headland. A white bar marks the end of an old vehicle track that comes in from Coles Bay. ATVs (quad bikes) can be hired at Coles Bay and taken along this track.

**5** Just past the bar go left through the bush and in a couple of minutes you will reach the granite lookout mentioned in the introduction.

## 5 Exploring Friendly Beaches

**6** When you are ready to return, walk along the vehicle track and take the first turn to the right which leads down to a disued campsite.

**7** Walk straight ahead to scale up a dune for a lovely view of the tranquil lagoon and its inhabitants. Return to the beach either via the road or across the dunefield to resume your journey.

**8** When you reach Saltwater Lagoon treat yourself to a small detour. Top a small dune on the northern side of the inlet and then follow the shore to its northernmost point, then head east back to the beach. This peaceful lagoon is fringed by unspoilt native vegetation. You will see many black swans, pelicans, plovers and herons to name just a few of the bird species to be found here.

**9** After your return to the beach you can spend some time exploring the various rocky outcrops and, at certain times of the year, the massive amounts of seaweed that are dropped here by the wave action. Then find your way back to the start point.

Cygnets

Friendly Point

## Tasmanian environment – Dunes

Coastal dunes have deep sandy soils that are very low in nutrients. They are often unstable and subject to erosion by wind and sea. Plants that have best adapted to these conditions are grasses, reeds and sedges. Their extensive underground stems and roots retain moisture and help to limit sand movement. In the more sheltered areas behind dunes, further away from the beach, a range of small annual plants often take foothold amongst the grasses and sedges. These are by necessity salt-tolerant and often include succulents. In more sheltered locations larger shrubs such as white correa, boobyalla and the highly adaptable *Banksia marginata* are able to establish themselves.

## Tasmanian industry – Seaweed

Marine plants such as wakame (*Undaria pinnatifida*) have been harvested, particularly in Asia, for thousands of years. In Tasmania this industry is relatively new. Here wakame is hand-harvested

from the cool waters off the East Coast from October to December. After washing and trimming it is simply dried in sheds. A drying and milling plant in Triabunna processes and exports the finished product. Another facility at Cambridge extracts fucoidans, using a unique coldwater extraction process, from edible seaweed. Fucoidans are added to some food or food products that are taken as supplements, in the belief that they benefit health or prevent disease. So next time you pass a pile of seaweed washed up on the shore, see if you can spot the dainty, fern-like leaves of wakame among all the usual bull kelp.

Limestone cliffs

# Maria Island

Maria Island became separated from the Tasmanian mainland when sea levels rose about ten thousand years ago, creating the Mercury Passage. Aboriginal people from the Oyster Bay tribe are said to have visited prior to white settlement using primitive canoes. Today the island is accessed by boat or ferry from Triabunna or by light aircraft. With the exception of Parks service vehicles, there are no cars on the island. Bicycles can be brought across on the ferry. The tiny settlement of Darlington has a permanent water supply from Bernacchis Creek, but the rest of the island is quite dry. There are several camping areas and some bunkhouse accommodation in the former penitentiary but no shops or other services, making for a very relaxed and peaceful atmosphere. As the 50-minute one-way ferry trip shortens the time you'll have to explore considerably, it is a good idea to camp for a night or two to be able to fully appreciate what the island has to offer. Parks passes apply to all walks on the island.

**Further information:** www.parks.tas.gov.au, Maria Island National Parks T (03) 6257 1420 Triabunna Visitor Information Centre T (03) 6257 4772

## Getting there:

Take the Tasman Highway (A3) to Triabunna. Follow visitor information sign (*i*) which leads to the harbour and ferry terminal.

**Ferry:** Operates twice daily in summer, crossing takes 40 to 50 mins. For bookings and timetable, call Maria Island Ferries T 0419 746 668, or East Coast Cruises T (03) 6257 1300.

**Plane:** Maria Island can also be reached by light plane. Call Par Avion on T (03) 6248 5390 for information on charter flights.

## The making of Maria Island

A number of natural and cultural events have shaped this beautiful, small island which is only about 20 kilometres long north to south and 13 kilometres wide west to east. An active fault which runs from Cape Boullanger in the north to Chinamans Bay in the south has downthrown (lowered the level of) the western half, including Darlington, by several hundred metres during early Tertiary times. An intrusion of a single large body of magma occurred during the Jurassic, forming Tasmania's signature rock, dolerite, which has since been most spectacularly exposed atop Bishop and Clerk and Mount Maria. Other layers of ancient rocks include a couple of different limestone layers which are the thickest in Tasmania and became important in the island's industrial era.

# Maria Island

Commissariats store

## Whalers, sealers and the convict eras

The first Europeans to settle and transform the island were sealers and whalers who established a whaling station. This was closed in 1825 when, to utilise the island's natural isolation, a penal colony for about 50 convicts was formed. However, due to mismanagement, it operated for only seven years.

The island enjoyed a period of quiet for ten years, before a second attempt to open the penal facilities was made. Existing buildings were enlarged and added to, to accommodate 600 convicts who mainly worked at growing crops such as potatoes, carrots, turnips, wheat, barley and hops and the quarrying of limestone to manufacture lime for mortar and brickmaking. It was eight years before the second station was closed in 1850.

## The industrial and farming eras

The turbulent times of the convict eras were followed by three decades of peaceful farming and grazing that created changes in flora and fauna. Finally, in 1884, a wealthy Italian silk merchant, Diego Bernacchi, saw the island's potential, leased the whole island and made his mark. He floated the Maria Island Company and transformed the island into a hive of activity. Fisheries, farms, vineyards and orchards were established, timber was exported and the thick limestone layers were quarried for the manufacture of cement. Even a holiday resort was incorporated. However the company went bankrupt during the depression in 1892.

Not to be deterred, Bernacchi formed a new company in 1920, National Portland Cement Ltd, again creating a flurry of activity raising the island's population to 800. Cement markets failed in 1930 and the company finally folded.

Coffee Palace

Forester Kangaroos

Cape Barren geese

## Wildlife sanctuary and National Park

Properties were gradually acquired by the government and the island was declared a wildlife sanctuary in 1971. It became Tasmania's only island national park a year later. There are now no permanent residents on the island with the exception of Park Rangers.

You may be able to add more detail to this colourful story during your stay on the island, as there is excellent interpretation to be found, particularly in the commissariat's store, the old mess building and the coffee-coloured coffee palace.

# 6 Bishop and Clerk

This is one of Maria Island's truly spectacular walks. Relatively easy to access, the small peak of Bishop and Clerk marks the northern end of the main mountain range on the island which also includes Mount Maria to the south. This walk leads you along the spectacular open, grassy Skipping Ridge (the rim of the Fossil Cliffs) and under the shady canopy of tall gums via a dolerite rock scree to the top of the craggy dolerite columns you can see from Darlington.

## At a glance

**Grade:** Medium/Hard

**Time:** 4 hr 30 mins

**Distance:** 9 km return

**Ascent/Descent:** 620 m/620 m

**Conditions:** Gravel road and grassy, exposed track followed by steep, rocky sections through bushland, a rock scree and a short, awkward climb from the base of a dolerite column to its top

### Finding the track

From the jetty on Maria Island go right past the island's oldest building, the convict-built Commissariat's Store, now a Visitor Information Centre. Cross the bridge over Bernacchis Creek towards the tiny settlement of Darlington. The third cottage on your right is the Park Rangers' office and marks the start of your walk

## Walk directions

**1** Turn left into the road signed *Bishop and Clerk* which leads past the Twelve Apostles – these are the foundations of workers' cottages built in the 1880s. The cottages were relocated in the 1930s to Maria Street in the Hobart suburb of New Town. Up ahead the distinctive, craggy outline of the dolerite-capped Bishop and Clerk will come into view above the trees.

**2** Soon you will walk beside Bernacchis Creek and the bush will become denser, especially on the creek bank where moisture-loving plants such as dogwood and prickly Moses prefer to grow. To the right you will find prickly box.

**3** Cross a small tributary to Bernacchis Creek before you reach an open area with a directional sign. Keep left at the sign and after fording Bernacchis Creek you will reach a crossroads.

**4** Go straight ahead and uphill on the grassed vehicle track following signage to Bishop and Clerk. The track leads up a gully through thinning bush, past blackwood trees and old quarry workings on the right. You may hear mountain jays (currawongs) calling and perhaps see a wedge-tailed eagle soaring above. Bishop and Clerk reappears as you near the top of the limestone cliffs and pass a warning sign.

## Tasmanian birdlife – Mountain Jay or black currawong (*Strepera fuliginosa*)

Although the Mountain Jay looks a bit like a crow or raven, this beautiful bird is endemic to Tasmania and belongs to a different species. It has yellow rather than white eyes and a hook on the end of its beak. It is shiny black with white tips on tail and wings and sings a beautiful song.

# 6 Bishop and Clerk

**5** Turn right to follow the spur named Skipping Ridge that leads along the rim of Fossil Cliffs – you will gain magnificent views across to your destination. Looking to the right you can also make out Darlington below and the prominent Three Thumbs Hills on mainland Tasmania. The vehicle track rises steeply towards a large blue gum and a little further a fine stand of she-oaks.

**6** A sign marks the end of the open area and as you enter the shady forest the track runs closer to the cliff edge with a steep drop to the right as well. A layer of she-oak needles forms a thick carpet underfoot and you will hear and see a number of birds. The track levels off briefly before another steep section. The deeper soils here support a dense forest with large gum trees overhead – blue gums, brown-top stringybark and white gum are all present. White gum is important for the survival of the forty-spotted pardalote, a very small, endangered bird endemic to Tasmania (on page 47).

**7** The vehicle track ends in a saddle and is replaced with a well-built foot track which curves left and becomes rocky as it follows the contour of the mountain. There are pink berry bushes in the understorey, and in spring you may see the beautiful white four-petalled flowers of clematis, a native climber. This area is a haven for many birds – the dense understorey also contains native cherries, cheeseberries and mountain pepper. Looking through the trees, views down to Cape Boullanger become wider.

**8** Next you will arrive at the base of a large dolerite scree, formed from toppled dolerite columns that have shattered and weathered through the ages.

**9** A well-built track, marked with posts, zigzags up the scree. Old stunted banksias grow here, and you will also see some rice flowers, or

CAPE BOULLANGER

Fossil Cliffs

Walk 8

Darlington Bay

Fossil Bay

Walk 7

Bernacchi

Reservoir Creek

Counsel Creek

MARIA ISLAND NATIONAL PARK

N

0    50

## Maria Island birdlife – Forty-spotted pardalote (*Pardalotus quadragintus*)

This tiny bird, one of the smallest, rarest birds in Australia, is sadly classified as endangered. Measuring just nine to ten centimetres it can only be found in eastern Tasmania. Bruny Island and Maria Island are both lucky to accommodate larger colonies of more than a hundred birds. The forty-spotted pardalote has a dull olive-green body with lemon yellow patches around the eyes and on its rump. Its wings are blackish with distinctive, small white dots – perhaps forty, though it's hard to tell! These birds are fussy. They live and feed in the treetops of dry eucalypt forests and woodlands, but only where white gum (*Eucalyptus viminalis*) grows, picking up a variety of insects, lerps (a protective insect coating) and manna (a sugary secretion produced by the tree in response to insect attack).

bushman's bootlaces, with their shiny, round leaves clutching hairy white stems.

**10** At the top of the scree you will soon see the distinctive dolerite columns of the summit appear before you.

**11** Keep right at an apparent Y-junction and follow the markers. After some more serious rock-hopping you will reach the first dolerite column, with an old Oyster Bay pine (*Callitris rhomboidea*), a tree that

only occurs on Tasmania's East Coast, growing at its base. A couple of rather tricky scrambles will get you to the top of the column for superb views and perhaps a well-earned rest before retracing your steps to the start point.

# 7 Oast House and Painted Cliffs Circuit

This is a leisurely walk through bushland past the historic ruin of an oast house to a spectacular outcrop of Triassic sandstone. You will return along a tranquil beach and the island's main road, where you are bound to see some of the island's friendly wildlife grazing in the cleared and previously farmed areas, to complete this lovely short circuit. It is worth obtaining the tidal information, which is displayed at the Commissariat's Store/Visitor Information Centre, prior to setting off on this walk, as the cliffs are best visited one hour either side of low tide.

## At a glance

**Grade:** Easy
**Time:** 2 hrs
**Distance:** 5.1 km circuit
**Conditions:** Gravel roads, short rocky section and well-made foot track, exposed near coast

### Finding the track

From the jetty on Maria Island go right past the island's oldest building, the convict-built Commissariat's Store, now a Visitor Information Centre. Cross the bridge over Bernacchis Creek towards the tiny settlement of Darlington. The third cottage on your right is the Park Rangers' office and marks the start of your walk

## Walk directions

**1** Walk straight ahead on the main gravel road which leads past a campground on the left. Back in 1842 this was the site of the Superintendant's Quarters.

**2** Keep right at a Y-junction to follow the signed track to Painted Cliffs. A panel with a map at the start of this track shows an outline of your walk. On your right are open paddocks, with the sea beyond, where you can often watch wallabies, kangaroos and Cape Barren geese grazing on the pasture. White-backed magpies and native hens also enjoy this environment. The track, lined with large radiata pines, crosses a watercourse as it leads uphill.

**3** Turn left at the next junction into an old disused vehicular track. This leads into a stand of tall blue gums with a very sparse understorey of native grasses. In the distance, to your left, you can see the craggy peaks of Bishop and Clerk. The understorey soon becomes denser. This is a peaceful place where the only sounds are distant waves and birdsong.

**4** The track curves to the right to descend towards Counsel Creek. She-oaks and prickly box grow here, and in late winter and spring common heath adds splashes of colour to the bush. Opposite a grassed area on the right you can see some evidence of serious wombat activity – you may even encounter a wombat, as they are plentiful here. Across the small paddock are views towards Orford and the Three Thumbs on the Tasmanian mainland. A couple of well-shaped blackwood trees stand at the end of the paddock.

**5** After passing the blackwoods, the curious ruins of the Oast House appear on the right (see box below). A blue sign marks the continuation of the track, which goes down through a small grassy clearing edged by large blackwoods and blanket bush towards Counsel Creek. The track swings right to cross a watercourse via a wooden footbridge and continues along a gravelled path, crossing a small marsh where sedges and ferns

## Tasmanian fauna – Wombat (*Vombatus ursinus*)

As their scientific name suggests, these solidly built marsupials are 'bear-like' with their coarse dark brown fur and broad, clawed paws. Wombats are largely nocturnal, but during winter they can sometimes be spotted sunbaking or

grazing during the day. They construct large burrows, up to 20 metres long. Although they appear slow, they can move at surprisingly high speeds when startled. Their diet consists of native grasses, herbs, shrubs and roots and their preferred habitat is heathland. Wombats give birth to one young joey which stays in the mother's pouch for about six months and gains independence at about eighteen months of age.

grow. Wombats will have left their brick-shaped calling cards on the track. You may in fact spot some wombats here – some of them are so placid, you need to be careful not to trip over them!

**6** Cross Counsel Creek on another small bridge and re-enter the forest. The track winds pleasantly through an understorey of saggs, bracken fern and blackwood as the coast gradually appears ahead.

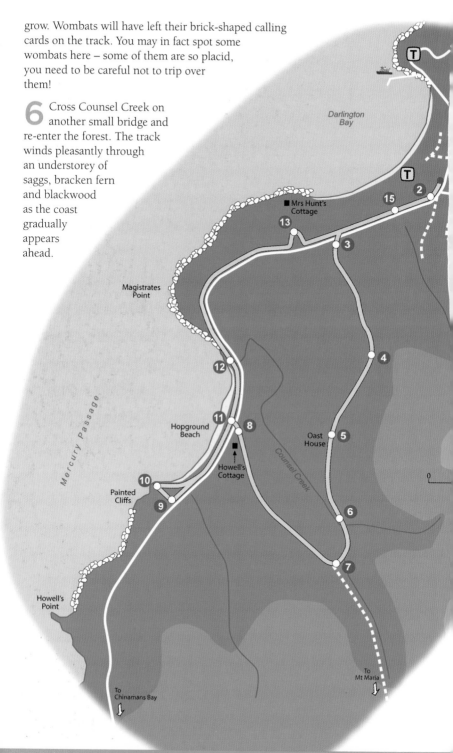

**7** Keep right at a T-junction where you meet the track that leads to Mount Maria. You can see a small cottage on your left and ahead a low rise known as Magistrates Point, with the main road to Darlington leading to its top. Walk around a large old conifer on the now sandy track to meet the main road from Darlington which goes to Chinamans Bay and the southern half of the island.

**8** Take a moment to look at the cottage on your left – it was inhabited by the Howell family who farmed this area in the early 1900s. Old packing cases were recycled to line its inside, and layers of newspaper and wallpapers with old-fashioned designs once covered the packing cases. A picnic table can be found under the pine trees.

**9** Continue southwards along the main road, crossing a small creek, and turn right into the signed Painted Cliffs track which leads through some large macrocarpa pines and down a set of wooden steps to Hopground Beach.

**10** Here you can admire the aptly named Painted Cliffs, which are to your left. The beautiful patterns are created by water, which percolates through the porous sandstone leaving an iron oxide band where it stops and dries. Another band starts when the process is repeated, and so on through the ages.

**11** To return to your start point, walk the full length of Hopground Beach. You may see oystercatchers, crested terns, pacific gulls and hooded plovers or even spot a sea eagle hovering above.

**12** Cross Counsel Creek, which forms a small lagoon here before it flows into the bay, and go straight ahead to join the main road to Darlington which you saw earlier.

Bernacchi Creek

Walk 6

LAND NATIONAL PARK

Painted Cliffs

# 7 Oast House and Painted Cliffs Circuit

From the top of Magistrates Point you can enjoy great views to Mount Maria and Bishop and Clerk to the right and across Mercury Passage to mainland Tasmania's east coast.

**13** Soon Mrs Ruby Hunt's cottage will come into view on your left. It was built in the 1900s and overlooks Darlington Harbour. Mrs Hunt operated a pedal wireless to link Maria Island to mainland Tasmania. Retrace your steps to the start point at Darlington which can be seen up ahead.

Mrs Hunt's Cottage

Painted Cliffs

## Maria Island history – Oast House

This curious structure dates back to the second convict era on Maria Island. It has had several functions according to need at the time. Initially it served as hop kilns to dry hops harvested from surrounding hop fields. Later, the original kilns were modified so that the building could be used for crushing grapes during the Bernacchi era. Finally it was turned into an abattoir, during the 1920s.

# 8 Quarries and Fossil Cliffs Circuit

Take a step back in time to Maria Island's first industrial era when the quarrying of limestone was in its heyday. You will initially follow Bernacchi Creek then climb to explore the old quarry sites. You will reach the spectacular views of Skipping Ridge (described in Walk 5) and return via the famous Fossil Cliffs where the Darlington Limestone was quarried.

Fossil Cliffs

## At a glance

**Grade:** Medium

**Time:** 2 hr 30 mins

**Distance:** 5.5 km circuit

**Ascent/Descent:** 60 m/60 m

**Conditions:** Gravel roads and well-made foot track, a short open non-tracked section; exposed for coastal areas

## Finding the track

From the jetty on Maria Island go right past the island's oldest building, the convict-built Commissariat's Store, now a Visitor Information Centre. Cross the bridge over Bernacchis Creek towards the tiny settlement of Darlington. The third cottage on your right is the Park Rangers office and marks the start of your walk

## Walk directions

**1** The first section of this walk is identical to Walks 6 and 9. Turn left into the signed Bishop and Clerk track which leads past the Twelve Apostles. These are the foundations of workers' cottages built in the 1880s. The cottages were relocated in the 1930s to Maria Street in the Hobart suburb of New Town. Up ahead the distinctive, craggy outline of the dolerite-capped Bishop and Clerk will come into view above the trees.

**2** Soon you will walk beside Bernacchis Creek and the bush will become denser, especially on the creek bank where moisture-loving plants such as dogwoods and the spiky acacia generally known as prickly Moses prefer to grow. To the right you will find prickly box.

**3** Cross a small tributary to Bernacchis Creek before you reach an open area with a directional sign. Keep left at the sign and after fording Bernacchis Creek you reach a crossroads.

**4** Turn right at the *Reservoir Circuit* sign and you will see an impressive brick ruin on your left, a few metres from the track. This is the engine house of a former cement works, where material from the old quarries was processed into lime. Take some time to inspect this interesting site.

**5** To continue your walk to the old quarries, return to the reservoir road and follow it along the bank of Bernacchis Creek through tall, wet forest with ferns and native currant bushes in the understorey.

**6** At the next junction go left and uphill on the access road to the quarries which NPWS occasionally still use today for track maintenance Here you can see the exposed layers of limestone that were used in the lime works. Walk to the far end of the workings past any stockpiles of gravel and locate a leafy, disused road which follows the contour of the hillside. This pleasant, short road leads through bushland that is a haven for birds, butterflies and animals. After passing some she-oaks you emerge into a small, grassy clearing where wombats and wallabies may be found grazing peacefully.

7 Although the road ends here, continue toward a large gum tree growing out of a heap of overburden gravel. Keep to the left of the gum to continue along the line of various old quarries taking care with uneven ground. The large area in the gully down on your left has been cleared for grazing and you will see the track to Bishop and Clerk leading through it towards the saddle up ahead. After passing through some prickly box and inspecting the last of the quarries, head across the clearing towards the coast and a directional and warning sign regarding hazardous cliff edges.

8 From here follow the *Fossil Cliff Circuit* signs. The grassy route that leads along the rim of Fossil Cliffs is marked

Convict Barn

Quarry

## Maria Island history – Engine House

On 10th September 1889 the foundation stone for Australia's first Portland Cement Works was ceremoniously laid. The two-storey brick ruin with arched windows and doors you see today was the engine house for the cement works. Twenty lime kilns were planned for construction behind the engine house but only five were subsequently constructed. A large brick home was erected for the works engineer at the same time.

Millers Cottage

on the ground, where a windmill once stood. The mill had a long tail pole which was moved around the circle by hand so that the mill would face the wind. Wheat and corn were ground here.

**12** Head to the right now to inspect the large convict barn that overlooks the harbour and is filled with historic wagons and farm machinery. Further west you can find the free settlers' cemetery before going downhill to join the main road back to your start point.

**13** If you have the time you can also explore the other ruins further south-east on this rise which include Bernacchi's former residence.

with white posts. It heads steeply uphill for a short distance and passes the remains of an old fence on the right, a relic from farming days, before going downhill. The small island you can see just offshore is Ile du Nord with Bird Rock on its right. In the distance you may be able to see Schouten Island and the Freycinet Peninsula. Access the cliffs after you cross a small gully.

**9** A track leads down to an excellent interpretive sign. You will be able to stand on the quarry floor – the quarried rock was transported from here by tramway to Darlington Harbour (remnants of tramway sleepers can still be found).

**10** Continue to follow the white marker posts, leaving the island's air strip to your right. Forester kangaroos, Bennett's wallabies, Cape Barren geese and Tasmanian native hens that have been introduced to the island are thriving on the poa grassland here. When you spot a cottage ahead and uphill near the bush to the left, begin to head towards it.

**11** This is the former Miller's Cottage. You can still see a large circle

## Maria Island environment – Permian rocks

Permian rocks on Maria Island include pebble conglomerate, sandstones, siltstones and two distinct layers of limestone. The oldest and therefore the lowest is known as Darlington limestone as seen along the Fossil Cliffs. Although at first touted as practically inexhaustible, it was fairly useless for cement production. Due to the large overburden of sandstone, eight to ten tons of rubbish had to be moved for every ton of limestone. The younger limestone, in a higher layer, is known as Berriedale limestone and you see it in the old quarries above Bernacchis Creek and the Engine House. During your walk past the latter you may notice that it contains impurities in the form of thin beds of clay and mudstone. The removal of these impurities also caused production costs of cement to rise and contributed to the demise of Bernacchi's empire.

Only a few building projects from the convict era remain on Maria Island. They include the Commissariat's Store near the modern jetty, the Penitentiary, now used for bunk accommodation, the Mess Room and the all important water reservoir, which you will visit on this walk. The Reservoir is still in use today as Darlington's main water supply.

This is a gentle, near-level stroll which leads through shady forest following the western bank of Bernacchis Creek upstream. You return via the eastern bank where you can inspect some interesting brick ruins from the late 1800s. The easy availability of water and

Darlington

dense vegetation in this area supports many birds and some friendly wildlife which you may be lucky enough to encounter along the way. Near the end of this walk many wallabies, kangaroos and Cape Barren geese can be observed grazing on the grass, particularly at dawn and dusk.

## At a glance

**Grade:** Easy

**Time:** 2 hrs

**Distance:** 6 km circuit

**Ascent/Descent:** 20 m

**Conditions:** Gravel roads and well-made foot track, mostly level and shady

### Finding the track

From the jetty on Maria Island go right past the island's oldest building, the convict-built Commissariat's Store, now a Visitor Information Centre. Cross the bridge over Bernacchis Creek towards the tiny settlement of Darlington. The third cottage on your right is the Park Rangers' office and marks the start of your walk

## Walk directions

**1** The first section of this walk is identical to the start of Walks 6 and 8. Turn left into the signed Bishop and Clerk track which leads past the Twelve Apostles. These are the foundations of workers' cottages built in the 1880s. The cottages were relocated in the 1930s to Maria Street in the Hobart suburb of New Town. Up ahead the distinctive, craggy outline of the dolerite-capped Bishop and Clerk will come into view above the trees.

**2** Go right into a gravel road at the next Y-junction to follow Bernacchis Creek which is on your left. Tall blue gums tower overhead with patches of sedge beneath.

**3** Keep left at a blue directional *Reservoir Circuit* sign, which points into a disused vehicle track with a leafy carpet, and follow the creek. The vegetation changes to include bracken fern and Acacia verticillata, commonly known as prickly Moses.

**4** The track dips down as it crosses a small tributary. It is cool and shady here and small interpretive signs name particular plants that appear along the track. These are *Acacia terminalis* (sunshine wattle), *Eucalyptus obliqua* (browntop stringybark) and *Allocasuarina littoralis* (bull oak). You can also find native cherry trees and dogwoods or blanket leaf in the understorey. A water valve and filter, which are part of the current water system, can be seen beside the track before you reach a short wooden footbridge across a watercourse.

**5** The track narrows here turning into a foot track as you pass

# 9 Convict Reservoir Circuit

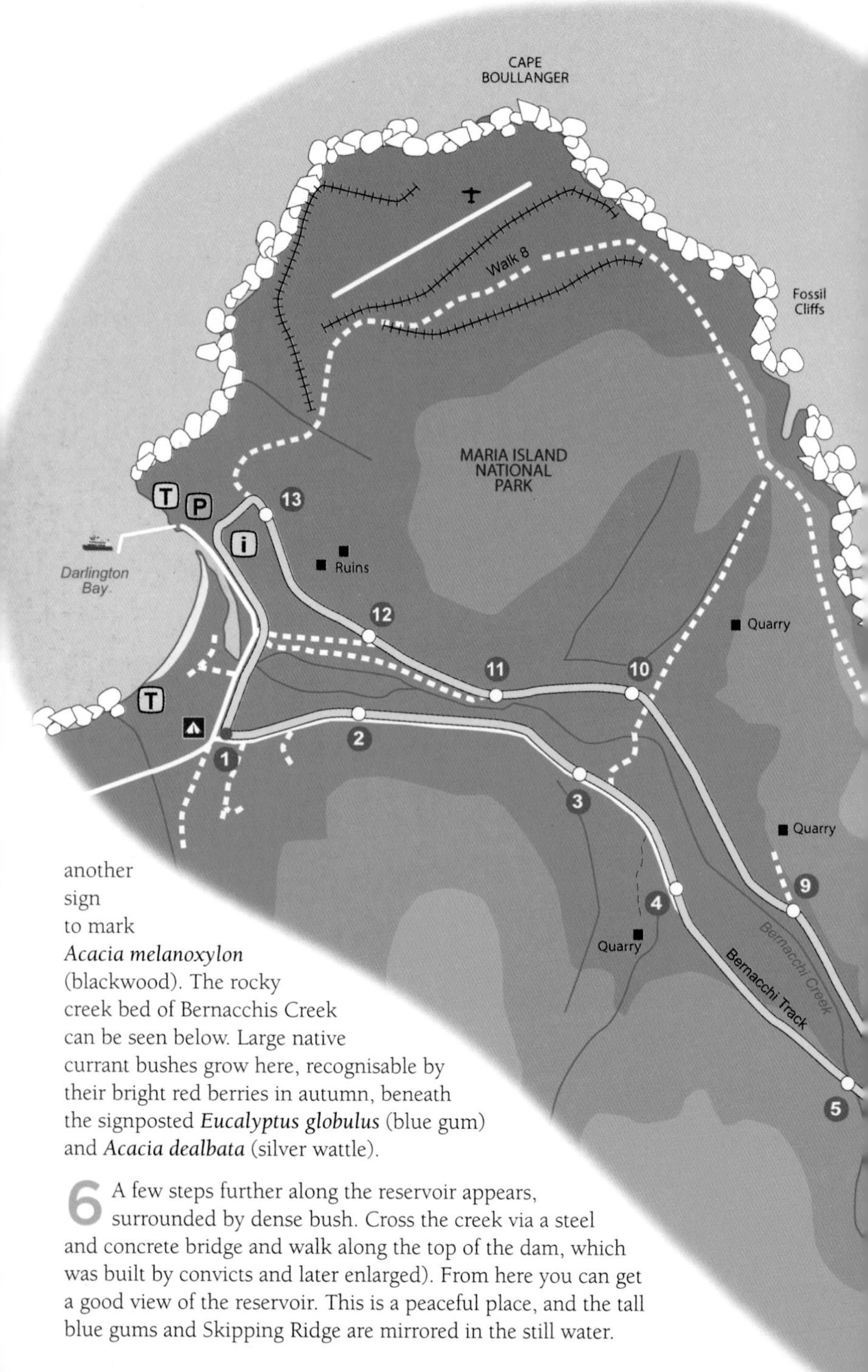

another
sign
to mark
*Acacia melanoxylon*
(blackwood). The rocky
creek bed of Bernacchis Creek
can be seen below. Large native
currant bushes grow here, recognisable by
their bright red berries in autumn, beneath
the signposted *Eucalyptus globulus* (blue gum)
and *Acacia dealbata* (silver wattle).

6 A few steps further along the reservoir appears,
surrounded by dense bush. Cross the creek via a steel
and concrete bridge and walk along the top of the dam, which
was built by convicts and later enlarged). From here you can get
a good view of the reservoir. This is a peaceful place, and the tall
blue gums and Skipping Ridge are mirrored in the still water.

**7** Turn left into a gravel road which runs along the opposite (north-eastern) bank of the creek, with the base of Skipping Ridge rising steeply on your right. The road slopes down gently making for easy going. You can spot the odd manfern under the tall trees down by the creek.

**8** In about five to ten minutes you will come to a junction. Keep left (the road to the right leads to major quarry workings – see Walk 8 for this interesting circuit). After a longish straight stretch of road you will spot an imposing brick ruin through the trees on your right. This is the Engine House of a former cement works, dating back to the Bernacchi era in

*Fossil Bay*

1887. The next track junction is nearby, in an open, well-clipped, grassy area which is maintained by wallabies that graze here at dawn and dusk. If the light is right you may be able to make out a tramline formation that runs from the Engine House westwards.

**9** Turn right to follow the road which immediately curves left, passing a couple more ruins. The nearest is the remains of the former Engineer's House (built in 1888) with only a bricked gateway and two tall chimneys left standing. A little further north, near the forest, stands a smaller brick workers' cottage and outhouse.

*Reservoir*

N
↑
0          250m

**10** Follow the road, with Bernacchis Creek now on your left. Blanket leaf, prickly box and poa grasses line the creek bank. The grassy understorey is a fine food source for wallabies, potoroos and wombats that can be seen grazing here. After about 200 metres Darlington comes into view.

# 9 Convict Reservoir Circuit

**11** Turn right at the next Y-junction to follow a grassy track which was once a tramline. Keep right as you pass a large blue gum, then head uphill towards a large conifer among ruins which include Bernacchi's former home.

**12** From here you have the option to head down towards the main road back to the ranger station and your start point, or to continue along the open, grassy crest of the hill towards a large convict-built barn which overlooks the harbour, before making your way back down to the main road and your start point.

Lime kilns

## Australian flora – The problem with dogwood

Scientific plant names often elicit groans from people who prefer to use common names. The common name means more to us, as it describes the plants in terms that we can readily understand. However, believe it or not, the botanical names create less confusion about which plant is actually seen and described. For example the name dogwood can refer to at least three different plants:

*Bedfordia salicina*, *Pomaderis elliptica* or *Pomaderis apetala*. Conversely, *Bedfordia salicina* has three common names: dogwood, blanket leaf and native willow. So should we fix the 'dogwood problem', or simply all just learn Latin and ancient Greek? For ease of reading, most of the plant names given in this guide are the common names. However there is a glossary of botanical names in the back for those who would like more information.

## Tasmanian birdlife – Cape Barren goose

These large grey geese with the 'high-vis green', waxy nostril patches (known as ceres) are rare worldwide but common on the offshore islands of southern Australia. They breed in tussocky, grassy or scrubby areas and were introduced to Maria Island as a refuge during the late 1960s and early 1970s.

# East Coast

From Swansea southwards to Dunalley, where only a bridge over a canal connects mainland Tasmania to the Forestier and Tasman Peninsulas, the sunny, friendly East Coast of Tasmania has much to offer. Visit the seaside villages of Swansea and Triabunna and explore the little known history of the Lisdillon Salt Works. Walk the flora rich hills of The Thumbs that dominate the landscape, enjoy pristine beaches at Orford and Marion Bay or marvel at the tall trees in the Wielangta Forest. The choice is yours; there is a great variety of walks to be found in this chapter.

# 10 Swansea Seaside Village

Halfway along Tasmania's East Coast, facing Great Oyster Bay, this historic seaside village's claim to fame is that it is situated in Australia's oldest rural municipality. The Swansea area enjoys the warmest and sunniest climate in Tasmania and it is therefore little wonder that its population of about 600 has the highest percentage of over 65-year-olds in Tasmania. It follows that the town has a very relaxed feel about it. You will enjoy walking its beautiful beach, around Waterloo Point with views across to Freycinet Peninsula and through the town to see some of its historic buildings while at the same time keeping fit so that you can better enjoy your own old age!

## At a glance

**Grade:** Easy
**Time:** 1 hr 30 mins
**Distance:** 4.8 km circuit
**Ascent/Descent:** 20 m
**Conditions:** footpaths, beach, little shade, some street crossings

**Further information:**
www.gsbc.tas.gov.au
**Getting there**
**Car:** 134 kilometres from Hobart on the Tasman Hwy (A3) or 133 kilometres SE of Launceston, park at Swansea Bark Mill and Museum at northern end of town

## Walk directions

**1** The original Bark Mill, where this walk begins, was established in 1885 and operated until the 1960s. It has been restored as a working mill. Bark from local black wattle trees (*Acacia mearnsii*) was once crushed and exported as an ingredient for tanning hides. You may wish to inspect the award-winning Bark Mill Museum and relax with a coffee or glass of wine in the same complex before or after this walk.

**2** From the car park go right to walk along the footpath of the Tasman Highway (Franklin Street) until you see a large 3-storey brick building named *Morris' General Store*. This was owned and run by the Morris family for over a hundred years. Carefully cross the street and walk past the store until you see a low dry-stone wall with a gateway. The tall symmetrical conifer trees you see here are the exotic Norfolk Island pines that tend to thrive in milder, coastal climes.

**3** Enter and go past a picnic and barbecue area on the left. Just before an outdoor theatre, step down to join a gravel path which leads past a children's playground to a public jetty from where you can enjoy the clear waters of the bay.

**4** Cross the jetty car park towards a *Great Short Walks* sign and go down to the beach to follow the shore. The small headland up ahead is Waterloo Point which carries the green lawns of a

very scenic nine-hole golf course with undulating, tree-lined freeways and spectacular views across Oyster Bay. You may have to step over some smelly bull kelp which tends to accumulate and turn into compost at the eastern end of the beach. Continue to follow the water's edge as it curves left and becomes pebbly.

**5** The Loontitermairre-lehoiner track begins just before a large blue gum at an interpretive sign about Aboriginal and colonial occupation of Waterloo Point. From here the gravel path snakes along the rocky foreshore past some novel tree stump seating, with the golf course now on your right. She-oaks and white correas grow here. Shortly you will reach Waterloo Point where a large slab of rock juts into the sea. At the top of the slab is a well-placed seat from where, weather permitting, you can enjoy uninterrupted views to Schouten Island on the right and Freycinet Peninsula on the left, recognisable by its craggy peaks – The Hazards.

**6** A little further along the track a sign explains who has dug the small holes into the sandy bank below the track!

Franklin St  
Shaw St  
Tasman Hwy  
Jubilee  
Beach  
Maria St  
Meredith House  
Noyes St  
River St  
Victoria St  
Plas Newyd  
Wellington St  
Julia St  
Bridge St  
SWANSEA  
Esplanade  
Schouten House  
Schouten Beach  
Waterloo Beach  
Waterloo Point Track  
Waterloo Point  
Swansea Golf Course

N  
0    250m

bank below the track! Soon you find yourself at the northern end of the Esplanade. This leads along Schouten Beach, where a rusty anchor is displayed near a panel that tells the very sad story about the drowning of six children from one family during a storm at sea in 1850.

**7** From the Esplanade take the first street to the right between two cemeteries. The row of ironbark gums are imports from the large island north of Tasmania. The Catholic cemetery is on the right and the general cemetery is on the left behind a dry stone wall. A large white headstone close to the street corner marks the grave of the six children mentioned above.

**8** Turn left into Waterloo Road which leads along the public golf course on the right. On your left, at the junction with Wellington Street, stands Schouten House, a Georgian mansion built in 1844. It was later sold to Mr Large (the father of the six drowned children) who had planned to run it as the Swansea Inn. However his tragic loss caused him to abandon the idea and Schouten House became a Grammar School for boys for only five years, after which time it was turned into a private residence once more. It is now a guest house.

**9** Turn left again to return to Schouten Beach and walk along it until you see a creek. Go right to follow the creek to Duck Park where some ducks will greet you with gusto. Pass a small footbridge and the extensive playgrounds, barbecue and picnic facilities, a small skate park and even an outdoor gym for adults. This may be a good spot to rest a while, especially if you have children in tow.

**10** Follow the esplanade as it curves to the right and joins Victoria Street (Tasman Highway). There are some lovely views along the flood plains of Saltwater Creek.

**11** Carefully cross the highway and go right, then left into Julia Street which rises steeply. From its highest point looking west you can see farmland in the foreground and the forested hills beyond.

**12** Turn right into Rectory Street. On your right, at the T-junction with Wellington Street, is the convict-built historic home 'Plas Newyd', which was built from sandstone and fieldstone for the Assistant Police Magistrate Lt. Alexander MacKenzie in 1834, and is the oldest home in town. The house was later used as a Church of England Rectory for 85 years and has since been in private hands.

**13** Go left into Wellington Street to its junction with Noyes Street. Straight ahead is a water tower and to the right the solid stone All

Saints Anglican Church which dates back to 1871. Diagonally across Noyes Street is Meredith House, built in 1853, which was originally named Laughton House. Its first occupant, Gordon Burgess, married a cousin of Louisa Meredith (see below) who ran a Grammar School there. It is thought that it was run as a brothel before it was turned into a maternity hospital and later into a guest house. The latter was run by the daughter of James Morris of Morris' General Store which you walked by earlier. The house's name was changed to Canberra Guest House when a niece of the owner

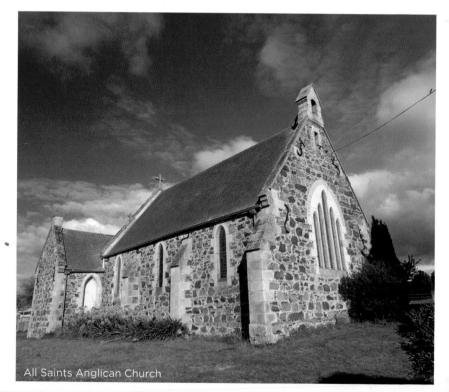

All Saints Anglican Church

took it up later. It became Meredith House in 1987 and is currently a guest house once more.

**14** Turn right into Noyes Street and go downhill past the town's History Room which opens on Tuesdays and Fridays from 1000 to 1600, the local police station and the impressive Municipal Office and Courthouse (c 1860) to its junction with Franklin Street (Tasman Highway). On the corner to your right is the Heritage Centre.

**15** Turn left and pass a restaurant and Post Office on your way back to the start point.

## Tasmanian history – Swansea & the Meredith family

Swansea was first settled in 1821 when George Meredith and his five children emigrated from England to Tasmania after his wife died unexpectedly. They received a grant to farm in the Oyster Bay area and they and other families that followed produced fruit, grain, wool, beef and sheep hides. Swansea was initially named Great Swanport and in 1860, when it became the first rural municipality in Tasmania, a black swan was depicted on the municipality's seal.

The Meredith's family home was 'Cambria', on the south bank of the Meredith River. George Meredith remarried and had seven more children. Several of his children became prominent and well-respected members of the community.

Charles Meredith, a son from his first marriage, was appointed colonial treasurer of Van Diemen's Land in 1857 and later Minister for Lands and Works. He held seats as a Member of the House of Assembly in various electorates. In total he was in parliament for almost 24 years. He was an advocate of free trade, and active in the preservation of native flora and fauna, perhaps through the influence of his wife Louisa Ann who was a well-known early Tasmanian author and artist. Her wildflower drawings won medals in exhibitions in Australia and overseas.

George's fourth son, John, was a magistrate at Swansea in 1855 and contributed greatly to the welfare of the district. He served in the House of Assembly for almost ten years as well.

# 11 Lisdillon Saltworks and Beach

Sited halfway between the coastal villages of Triabunna and Swansea, the Lisdillon salt works is one of only two early salt manufacturing works in eastern Australia where substantial remains can still be found. You can learn some intriguing facts about Tasmania's early history and combine this with a peaceful stroll along a beach and around a small headland in this easy, almost level, walk. Part of this walk traverses private farmland with kind permission from the owner, so please respect the land and animals as you would your own.

Lisdillon Salt Works

## At a glance

**Grade:** Easy

**Time:** 2 hrs

**Distance:** 5.5 km circuit

**Conditions:** Beach and coastal with little shelter; short section along road

**Further information:** Parks and Wildlife Service, Coles Bay
T (03) 6257 0107

## Getting there

**Car:** 114 kilometres from Hobart on the Tasman Hwy (A3), cross Little Swanport River then Boomer Creek. Take the next turn to the right into Saltworks Road. At 1.5 kilometres turn left into the short access lane opposite Cotton Drive to salt works site, and park in the car park

## Walk directions

**1** At the car park, in front of the ruins of the former salt works, you will find some interesting panels about the likely construction and operation of the works. The land you are standing on was once part of the large Lisdillon estate. The main area with the salt works ruins was returned to the Crown in 1983 and is now managed by Parks and Wildlife Service as part of a coastal reserve. You can see some evidence of the conservation work that was undertaken to prevent further deterioration of the ruins. Mismatched sawn sandstone was used deliberately to stabilise the structure to make it easier to identify the original stonework.

**2** Begin your walk by following the channel to the windmill site (as per point 2

on the interpretive sign). Here you may still be able to find where the windmill was anchored in the rock.

**3** Carefully make your way down the rocky slope towards the beach and continue northwards along it. Many shore birds nest in the dry sand in and along the dunes in this area from September to March. You can avoid disturbing them or stepping inadvertently on their well-camouflaged eggs by walking along the wet sand near the water – which, luckily, is also firmer and easier to walk on. Some of the birds you may encounter are the tiny hooded plover, the red-capped plover, pied oystercatcher, little tern and fairy tern.

**4** You will pass a very small rocky outcrop near the entry of a watercourse and some larger rocks a little further on. To the left, above the dunes, you can see the adjoining farmland, where sheep often graze peacefully.

**5** It is not far to the small rocky headland with bright orange lichen growing on some of the larger rocks. Small rock pools can be explored here. When you reach a small gulch, carefully step over the low fence to your left then return towards the coast to continue along the next small beach. The landmass across

# 11 Lisdillon Saltworks and Beach

the sea to the east is the Freycinet Peninsula with Schouten Island to its south.

**6** Go up the dune at the opposite end of the beach and skirt around the strainer post at the corner of a paddock, then continue along the grassy bank. When you reach the opposite corner of the paddock, step over the low plain wire fence on your right to continue along the farm boundary, avoiding the rocky section of the shore. Make your way down to the next beach.

**7** Shortly a derelict jetty will come into view and you will soon reach the wooden pylons that remain. The jetty is not far from the mouth of the Lisdillon Rivulet and just south of Mitchells Reef which is a lovely spot to explore or perhaps have a bite to eat before returning to the Saltworks site for the second section of this walk.

**8** From the salt works car park go right and walk along the access track to its junction with the Saltworks Road.

**9** Turn left and follow the gravel road down to the small bay in the Little Swanport Estuary lined with blue gums. Take the grassy track closest to the waterline which leads around to the jetty.

**10** Pass the jetty and continue along the shore. A sandspit which lies in Little Swanport will come into view, where pelicans and a number of shore birds can be seen sunning themselves or lazing about. Migratory birds often use this spot to rest and it is enjoyable to watch them.

**11** Continue along the road, or nearer the shore if you prefer, until you reach a narrow foot track. This leads up through a rehabilitation area to the top of a small headland which carries a particularly healthy stand of she-oaks. From its highest point there are views across Great Oyster Bay to Freycinet Peninsula.

**12** The foot track rejoins the vehicular track and you can continue along it back to the salt works.

## Tasmanian history – Lisdillon

James Radcliff was a bachelor from Belfast who arrived in Tasmania in 1830 to settle on Lisdillon where he built a stone homestead and outbuildings. He farmed the northern part of the estate and established the salt works about two and a half kilometres south of the homestead on forty acres of land that was cleared for the purpose.

John Mitchell became the subsequent owner of Lisdillon. He was a surveyor and came from England in 1837. He was initially appointed as superintendent of the convict establishment for boys at Point Puer on the Tasman Peninsula and served in this capacity for some eleven years. Six years later he acquired Lisdillon and brought out eight or nine families from England as tenant farmers for the estate. A store, church, school room and post office were built to cater for the small settlement's needs. Mitchell later expanded his operations to include the neighbouring property 'Mayfield' and other real estate in the area. John Mitchell died in 1880 and left his properties to his son Mark who sadly died in 1896 from serious injuries he sustained in a fall from a horse. By the early 1900s the tenant farmers were removed and the property turned into a larger grazing operation with all the buildings falling into disrepair.

Lisdillon had two more owners, Sir Henry Jones and John Hood, before it was acquired by the Cotton family from nearby 'Kelvedon' in the 1950s. Lisdillon remains in their hands to this day.

## Tasmanian history – Quakers

Francis and Anna Maria Cotton emigrated with their family from England in 1829. They belonged to the Society of Friends (Quakers). Kelvedon, alternating with Hobart and later with Launceston, became a main centre for monthly meetings for worship.

Central to the Quaker religion is the belief that Christian qualities are more important than Christian dogmas. They are peace loving people who embrace all of humanity with love and tolerance.

Quakers were few in numbers and it was soon realised that education would be the key to ensuring their survival. After five failed attempts in the mid-nineteenth century by various private members of the society to set up a school in Hobart, they were finally successful with The Friends' School opening in 1887. The school offered co-education (the first in the country) with much emphasis on Natural Sciences alongside the usual subjects. Today The Friends' School is the only Quaker school in the southern hemisphere and the largest in the world. Quaker and non-Quaker children from all over the world attend.

# 12 Triabunna

It is thought that the town's name comes from the Aboriginal name for native hen. Triabunna is the largest township on the East Coast and one of Tasmania's oldest towns. It was once a garrison for the penal colony of Maria Island which lies only about 15 kilometres to its south-east and can be reached by ferry from Triabunna in about 40 minutes. Today Triabunna is a small working port and the home of the controversial woodchip mill. A pleasant hour or so can be spent on this easy walk around a town with a population of fishermen and timber workers that is still relatively unaffected by mass tourism.

## At a glance

**Grade:** Easy

**Time:** 1 hr 30 mins

**Distance:** 4.4 km circuit

**Conditions:** Footpaths, road verges and foot tracks in open, exposed sections, some road crossings

**Further information:** Triabunna Visitor Information Centre
T (03) 6257 4772

### Getting there

**Car:** 88 kilometres from Hobart on the Tasman Hwy (A3), turn off from highway into Vicary Street. Turn right into Charles Street, right again into Esplanade and park

**Bus:** Tassielink, T (03) 6230 8900

Triabunna Wharf

## Walk directions

**1** Your walk begins in this charming wharf area where you can see the local fishing fleet who fish for scale fish, crayfish, scallops and abalone. A few small ferries that service Maria Island are also tied up here. You can take a little time to inspect the visitor centre (open daily from 1000 to 1600), which overlooks the wharf area, and the Seafarers Memorial that adjoins it as you go north along the esplanade. There are also some picnic tables and barbecue facilities in this narrow parkland.

**2** Continue along the wharf and the foreshore towards the bridge across the wide estuary of several creeks.

**3** Go right across the bridge for a small side trip into and around a little park on the other side which has a small skate park and an array of historic farming equipment and from where you can get a particularly good overview of the port and the village beyond. The Spring Bay Hotel, the large white building which dominates the waterfront, dates back to 1838. To your left are views across Spring Bay with the rolling hills of The Thumbs in the background.

**4** Recross the bridge and enter the Penguin Walk across the street on the right, marked by a couple of suitably painted rocks. Follow this foot track that leads along the riverbank. You will pass the rear of the Municipal Council Chambers.

**5** Go past the end of a rail fence along a dog exercise area and a seat that overlooks the wide, reedy estuary. You can hear the calls of, and sometimes see, plovers (masked lapwings), native hens, oystercatchers and other birds that nest in this area. A few clumps of eucalypts have been planted along the path to provide shade and shelter.

**6** A few minutes along another seat occupies a vantage point from where you can look across the estuary to the eastern half of the township. The road skirting the grassy hillside opposite to the left is Freestone Point Road which leads past seafood and seaweed processing plants (see Friendly Beaches walk) to the Triabunna Woodchip Mill.

**7** Shortly you will be able to watch pelicans happily fishing in the shallow waters. The track curves left and away from the water as you exit the reserve.

**8** Turn left into Victoria Street and continue your walk along it. At its intersection with Henry Street sits Cuffs Cottage on

your left. Also known as Blakes Cottage it was built circa 1866 and named after the shoemaker Thomas Cuff. Diagonally opposite is St Anne's Catholic Church and cemetery which was opened in 1869, as is proudly displayed on its stuccoed gable end.

**9** Continue along the lovely, wide, grassy verge of Victoria Street, with small paddocks on either side. At its intersection with Charles Street, you will find a general cemetery

on the left and tennis courts and sports grounds on the right. The cemetery contains some very old graves including that of Charles Meredith, the son of the Honourable C.M. Meredith (see box for Swansea walk, Walk 10).

**10** Go left into Melbourne Street, pass the childcare centre, and turn right into Franklin Street. About 100 metres along

on the right stands the sandstone building of St Mary's Anglican Church, not far from the Tasman Highway which begins to curve towards the coast here. The church was built in 1881 from stone that was quarried locally at Oakhampton just north of Triabunna.

**11** Return to Melbourne Street and turn right passing the District High School to where the

78

old school building from Maria Island (dating back to 1868) was relocated to form part of the modern school buildings. You will come to the junction with Vicary Street, which is the town's main centre of activity. The small weatherboard building on your right is the old post office which is now an online access centre.

**12** Turn left into Vicary Street passing Art Spaces (well worth a look) to the local hardware store on the corner of Vicary and Charles Streets. You can enter the store and ask to please be shown the original, lovingly restored, five-horse coach that was licensed in 1860 to run along the Old Coach Road from Hobart for 70 years.

**13** Continue your walk by walking back along Vicary Street, then carefully cross it just before the Triabunna Hall (built in 1912). You will pass a Backpackers hostel and tiny caravan park and the even tinier police station.

**14** Cross the Esplanade to locate a foot track between a large gum tree and a footbridge. Follow this pleasant foreshore trail with views to Maria Island, with the distinctive, jagged dolerite columns of Bishop and Clerk, on the horizon. An interpretive sign near the end of the trail informs you about the small 'Dead Island' in the bay which was used as a cemetery between 1847 and 1867.

**15** The trail will take you back to your start point at the wharf. From here you can take a quick look at the historic Spring Bay Hotel and a little further along, in Charles Street you will find the old barracks still standing in a small paddock with an interpretive sign across the street to tell you about their history.

**16** This concludes your walk. Return to your start point and perhaps call into the nearby visitor centre to chat to the friendly staff there.

## Tasmanian history – Triabunna woodchip mill

Since its establishment in the early 1970s for the purpose of exporting eucalypt chips, mainly to Japan, the mill has been controversial. Initially the mill processed waste wood from sawmills and logging operations, but later large areas of forest were clear felled to meet the increasing demand from the Japanese market. During the 1980s more woodchips were exported from Tasmania than from all other Australian states combined.

Tasmania's community became divided. One half claimed that the mill provided employment, and that the old rotten forests were being revived through the process of clear felling followed by regeneration burns. The other half of the community bemoaned the loss of irreplaceable old growth forests at bargain basement prices. By 2010 the price for woodchips had dropped severely and the mill was closed temporarily in April 2011, creating a major unemployment problem for the people of Triabunna. In a surprise move, two conservation-minded entrepreneurs and philanthropists bought the mill in July 2011 with the ultimate plan to develop the area as a tourist destination.

Old Barracks and Stables, Triabunna

# 13 Shelly Beach to Spring Beach

The township of Orford straddles the estuary of the Prosser River between the hills of The Thumbs and the shore of Spring Bay. It was built as a station for the convicts who constructed the road to the East Coast. However its main claim to fame was the huge quarry of high quality sandstone at Shelly Point. You will pass the quarry site during this lovely coastal walk and may wish to take the small side trip down to it. Other highlights of this walk include views across to Maria Island, which is only fifteen kilometres away, and a colourful array of wildflowers during spring and summer.

## At a glance

**Grade:** Easy

**Time:** 1 hr 45 mins plus 20 minutes to view the sandstone quarry

**Distance:** 6.4 km return

**Conditions:** Good wide track, mostly gravelled. Sheltered and shady, unfenced cliff sections not suitable for small children

**Further information:** Triabunna visitor information centre, T (03) 6257 4772.

## Getting there

**Car:** From the south take the Tasman Highway (A3) to Orford. Turn right into the main street (Charles St./Rheban Rd) at bridge. If travelling from the north, cross bridge and drive straight ahead for about 1.9 kilometres, turn left into Jetty Rd then right into East Shelly Rd. After 0.6 kilometres turn left towards public boat ramp to park

**Bus:** Tassielink, T (03) 6230 8900

## Walk directions

**1** Your track begins to the right (east) and leads along the bay with the foreshore to your left and the back boundaries of shacks and homes on your right.

**2** Some blue gums stand in a grassy area with boobyalla and pigface growing beneath as you pass an interesting boat shed, a pump station, a beach access and a jetty. Magpies can often be seen here.

**3** The shore becomes rocky as you reach a second jetty and slipway with a disused rusty winch and a very rustic old boatshed. Some taller gums with an understorey of hop bush, coastal wattle, she-oak and young Oyster Bay pines grow in a short

Magpie

section of dirt track as you near Luther Point at the end of East Shelly Beach Road. Here you will find a clear spot from where you can get a good view of Maria Island.

**4** The track rises slightly as it leads, closely in some places, along the edge of unfenced cliff tops. Maria Island remains visible to the east and looking northwards you can also make

out Freestone Point with the lighthouse at Triabunna.

**5** You will pass through a cleared area where in spring and summer you may be able to find many beautiful wildflowers, such as trigger plant, black-eyed Susan, common heath, rosy baeckea, running postman and many dainty little orchids. Some patches of 'garden escapes' such as diosmas and lilies, as well as a few 'foreigners' imported from interstate, can also be spotted by the keen gardener or horticulturist.

N

0    500m

West Shelly Rd

Jetty Rd

East Shelly Rd

Prosser Bay

Shelly    Beach

**5** Luther Point

**1** **2** **3** **4**

**6**

**7** Quarry Point

**8**

Charles St / Rheban Rd (C320)

ORFORD

**9**

**10** Spring Beach

# 13 Shelly Beach to Spring Beach

**6** After passing through a patch of larger trees and shrubs you will reach a large blue gum which serves as a viewing point to the massive sandstone face of an historic quarry up ahead on Shelly Heights.

**7** You can add a small side trip to your walk at this stage to visit the quarry floor beneath a fine stand of Oyster Bay pines. Allow about twenty minutes extra time for a bit of a look around. Locate a steep, rough, rocky track about seven metres from the large blue gum (waypoint 6) which joins an older track that has had a tree fall across it. Follow the track down. The sea has claimed the jetty that was once there, but you can still see a few hand-cut stone blocks that have been left behind.

**8** Return to the main track which leads along a sandy section with another garden-like area, this time containing bracken fern, grass trees and white flowering candles. Many narrow side tracks, leading from houses along the coast join the main track. You will pass a small lookout area from where you will be able to see Spring Beach,

Trigger Plant

Running Postman

## Tasmanian history – Orford Quarries

Quarrying began in the 1850s. The cut sandstone was rolled down the steep slope to the cliff face jetty to be loaded on ships. The high quality sandstone was chiefly used in the construction of public buildings in Southern Tasmania and Melbourne. The quarry closed in 1876 causing the population of Orford to shrink drastically. By 1910 only about twelve shacks remained in the township.

your destination. If you are lucky you may encounter a sea eagle or two in this area. The dead gum trees you can see here are a legacy of a long and severe drought prior to 2010.

**9** Soon you will find a very basic bench seat at a lookout point down on your left. It was erected by a local resident and overlooks Maria Island and Spring Beach. It is a lovely spot to rest.

**10** The track descends down to Spring Beach from here via a few sections of wooden steps and emerges by an old wooden boat shed. Perhaps you can take a break at the beach before you retrace your steps to the start.

Orford Quarries

## Tasmanian environment – Oyster Bay pine (*Callitris rhomboidea*)

This is one of a number of Tasmanian endemic pine species. It can be found in dry sclerophyll forests, grassy forests or heaths along the east coast of Tasmania and the Furneaux Group of islands. It prefers rocky areas with a low fire frequency. Oyster Bay pines are drought adapted with their sparse foliage. The 'needles' are actually photosynthesising stems with tiny leaves that look like brownish scales.

# 14 The Three Thumbs

The Three Thumbs are a prominent feature in the landscape of Tasmania's East Coast. They can be spotted from as far away as Maria Island, Triabunna and the Tasmanian Bushland Garden at Buckland. For those who seek solitude, expansive coastal views and bushland rich in species, this walk is one not to be missed.

## At a glance

**Grade:** Easy/Medium

**Time:** 2 hrs 30 mins

**Distance:** 4.5 km circuit

**Ascent/Descent:** 294 m

**Conditions:** Rocky bush track under tree canopy. Three minor ascents/descents

## Getting there

**Car:** From the south take the Tasman Highway (A3) to Orford. Turn right into the main street (Charles St/ Rheban Rd) at bridge. From north, cross bridge and drive straight ahead. At 1 kilometre turn right into Wielangta Road currently signed *Quarry*. Follow signage to The Three Thumbs Lookout (about 5 kilometres) along a gravel road, and park

## Walk directions

**1** From the lookout, walk back down the road for 200 metres to the *Three Thumbs Track 2 hrs return* sign which points up the steep rocky track that leads off the outside curve of the access road.

**2** After a short climb through dense vegetation which includes an unusually large number of cheeseberry bushes the track levels off and follows the ridge top. Depending on the time of the year you may see needlebush, common heath, dusty daisybush, slender speedwell, guinea flower, blue love creeper and *Caladenia* orchids in flower, to name just a few. Many birds are attracted to these rich pickings and you may hear them as you make your way. Tall gums overhead complete the picture.

**3** You will soon cross a saddle before climbing up the first 'thumb' or rocky hump. Small rock cairns begin to appear as markers along the track and are easy to

follow. From the top of the first 'thumb' you will be able to see the coast which is only four kilometres away as the crow flies (providing the weather is fine). The township of Triabunna, Freestone Point, Spring Bay, Orford with the Prosser River flowing into the sea and Maria Island are laid out in front of you as on a map.

**4** Ignore a green *Forest Track* sign and any marking tapes and continue to follow the cairned route dotted with the occasional red paint splotch, which now climbs the second 'thumb' which can be seen up ahead.

**5** As you descend into the saddle you will pass through a large patch of Tasmanian blanket bush.

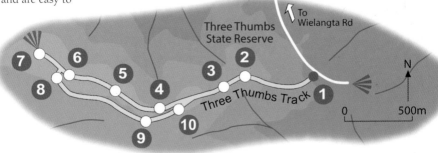

**6** A sign down in the saddle marks the turn-off to the Forest Track on the left, which will be your return route. The ascent to the last of the 'thumbs' takes only five to seven minutes and is well worth the effort. Kangaroo fern can be found alongside the track as you climb to the small rocky plateau, where you will find a trig, and a little further along, a large, partly destroyed rock cairn.

**7** The summit lends itself for a spell to take in the wide, panoramic views of the coast with Strawberry Hill in the foreground.

**8** Return to the Forest Track junction and go right to follow this loop which goes down steeply through tall dense forest of *Eucalyptus obliqua* and *Eucalyptus delegatensis* with an understorey dominated by an unusually thick stand of blanket bush and mountain pepper. You may hear the distinctive call of the mountain jay in this area.

**9** The track gradually curves left through the tall understorey and turns into a taped route. Take care not to lose the track markers (they come in various ages and colours, such as yellow, pink or blue) in this area. You may need to climb over a few cut or fallen logs before the vegetation becomes drier and sparser allowing you to see the route more clearly with the first 'thumb' coming into view on your left.

**10** The track heads to the first saddle you crossed on your way up. The junction with the main ridge track is fairly indistinct, but you will soon see the rock cairns you followed up earlier. This is where you turn right to retrace your steps to the lookout and start point.

Rock cairn

## Tasmanian flora – Mountain pepper (*Tasmannia lanceolata*)

Mountain pepper, or Tasmanian pepperberry, with its distinctive crimson stems, grows in high rainfall areas of Tasmania. The shrub can be up to five metres tall. Male and female flowers are borne on separate plants. The fruit is a small shiny black berry which was used by indigenous Australians as a medicine and condiment and by early settlers as a pepper and spice replacement. It has found its way back into modern cuisine. Leaves or berries, either fresh or dried, are often added to gourmet foods such as cheeses, mustards, dressings, breads and rolls, hamburgers and pates. Mountain pepper is also used by some restaurants to replace ordinary pepper to give a 'bush tucker' flavour. It is much stronger than normal pepper.

## Tasmanian flora – Cheeseberry (*Cyathodes glauca*)

This beautiful understorey shrub can grow to three metres in height and is endemic to Tasmania. Its botanical name describes it well – from the Greek kyathodes meaning cup-like – and refers to the shape of the 6 mm white flowers carried on the ends of its branches. Glauca means bluish green, the colour of the underside of its spiky leaves which cluster around the branches giving the shrub its distinctive look.

Three Thumbs Track

# 15 Wielangta Walk

The settlement of Wielangta was established in the early 1900s around a saw milling enterprise. At its peak the mill employed around one hundred men, but operation ceased in 1924 when all the timber had been cut down. Fire destroyed the settlement in 1928, and only a few small relics remain. This track takes you through cool, tall forest, managed by Forestry Tasmania, along part of the old tramway, following the course of the fern-lined Sandspit River. You may wish to arrange for a pick-up by car at the Wielangta Road end, but you would miss 1½ hours of this relaxing return walk.

## At a glance

**Grade:** Easy/Medium
**Time:** 3 hrs
**Distance:** 5.7 km return
**Ascent/Descent:** 100 m/100 m
**Conditions:** Shady and sheltered, easy climbs, a couple of creek crossings and a few fallen trees across the track. No track markers but track mostly easy to follow. Gaiters or long trousers recommended

### Getting there

**Car:** From Hobart take the Tasman Hwy (A3) to Sorell, then the Arthur Hwy (A9), turn left towards Kellevie and Nugent (C335). Follow signage to Wielangta Forest and park at Sandspit picnic area 14.2 kilometres from Arthur Hwy turn-off

## Walk directions

**1** Cross the picnic area down to the signposted track entry by a large tree stump with some interpretive signage about the history of the Wielangta settlement. Wooden steps lead down into the mixed forest of rainforest and eucalypt species.

**2** Cross a small tributary to the Sandspit River and go uphill then left and downhill along an old log drag line which leads to the tramway.

**3** Cross another tributary and keep left to continue downhill on a different drag line. Native currants and ferns can be

Sandpit River Crossing

## Tasmanian fauna – Wallabies

Only two species of wallaby are found in Tasmania. One is the **Bennett's wallaby** which occurs on mainland Australia from south-eastern Queensland to Victoria and South Australia as well. It is also known as red-necked wallaby (*Macropus rufogriseus*), because of the reddish colouring of its neck fur.

The other is the **Rufous wallaby** a.k.a. the Tasmanian pademelon (*Thylogale billardierii*). Due to its two common names, people often believe erroneously that these refer to two separate wallaby species.

Tasmanian wallabies can be distinguished by shape and size. The Bennett's can grow to 80 cm tall whereas the Rufous only reaches about 60 cm overall. The former is related to and looks like a kangaroo and the latter is a much stockier build with a shorter tail. Both can commonly be found in bushland adjoining cleared areas where they feed on grasses and herbs. The pademelon prefers denser bush and will include shrubs in its diet. They are nocturnal and shelter in the bush during the day.

seen to grow in these moist conditions.

**4** The track curves to the right, leading through tall bracken fern, cutting grass, shrubby native olive, stinkwood and mosses. You may also note the beautiful trunks of silver wattles.

**5** As you begin a steeper climb, the track becomes partly overgrown with ferns before another minor creek crossing.

**6** Directly you will reach a small, rocky clearing on a slope. The main item of cultural heritage to be found here is the wreck of an old 1950s

Vanguard sedan. Continue to a Y-junction where you will find the beginning of the old tramway.

**7** Keep left and follow it down to the Sandspit River. You can catch glimpses of it on your left as it tumbles over smooth boulders. Some of the manferns here are forming a canopy above your head as you make your way through ferny, slightly overgrown sections alternating with more open lightly timbered areas.

**8** Cross the Sandspit River via some flat boulders and a log, then keep left up the river bank to rejoin the

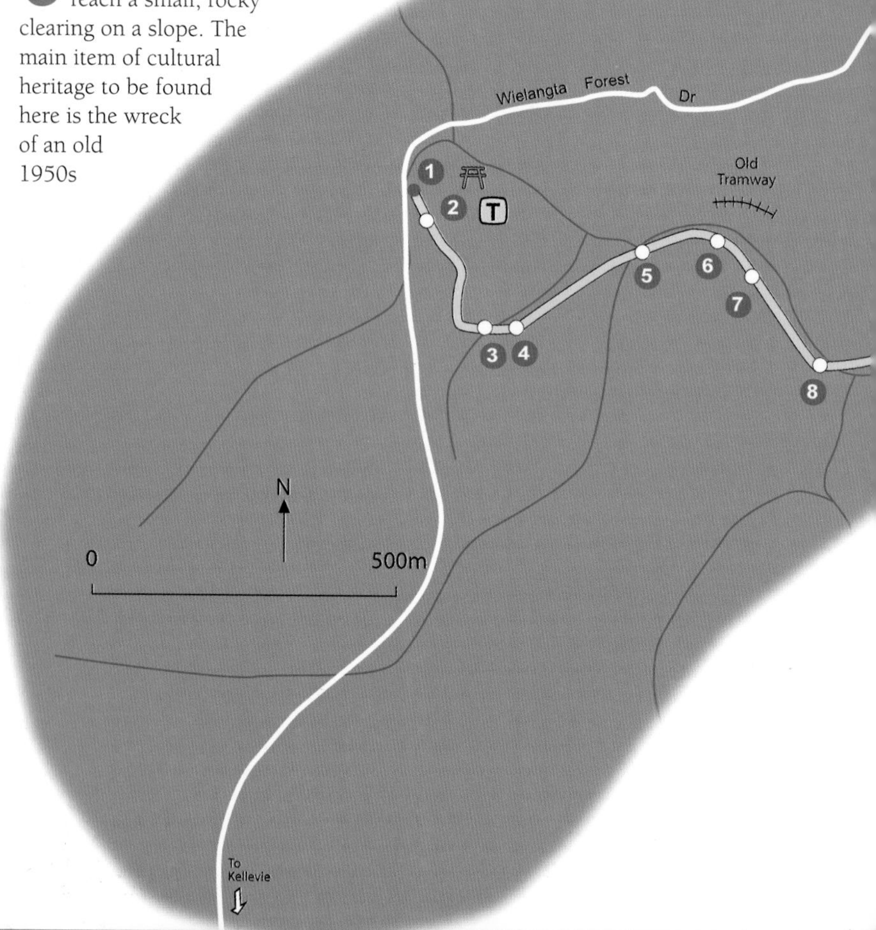

Sandspit
Forest Reserve

Wielangta  Forest    Dr

Old
Tramway

1 🏓
2 T

5  6
7

3 4

8

N

0          500m

To
Kellevie

To
Orford

P

11

■ Memorial

10

River

9

Sandspit

track which now leads through a wider river valley with dry sclerophyll forest. A short 'obstacle course' over some fallen trees and branches follows as the track rises gently along the contour, leaving the river below to your right.

**9** A short boardwalk takes you across a wet spot back towards the river. The track widens. Keep a lookout for Rufous wallabies (pademelons) which can be found along the track.

**10** Carefully cross a bridge with partially collapsed decking over a small watercourse. Shortly you will see an open area with blue gums and silver wattle. Skirt along its right side to avoid the thick stand of perennial thistles that have infested this area.

**11** Finally the track emerges at the Wielangta Road. A memorial to Alex Leonard Swan can be found on your right just before the road. The little boy died as a result of an accident with explosives. Retrace your steps to the picnic area to once more enjoy the lovely forest atmosphere.

# 16 The Long Spit to Marion Bay

A privately owned nature reserve divides the sheltered mudflats of Blackman Bay from Marion Bay's surfing beaches. If you love semi-deserted beaches this walk is definitely for you as there is a high chance that you will have all three kilometres of it to yourself and the birds; the area is frequented by large numbers of shore birds such as pied and sooty oystercatchers, fairy and little terns, hooded plovers and red-necked stints. Highlights also include a beautiful array of shells to be found and of course wide views across the bay.

## At a glance

**Grade:** Easy

**Time:** 2 hrs

**Distance:** 6.6 km circuit

**Conditions:** Exposed to sun and wind, walk along beach with return by 4WD track

### Getting there

**Car:** Take the Arthur Highway (A9) as far as Copping and turn left. Follow signage to Marion Bay and keep right at a Y-junction to go over a bridge then along intertidal mudflats to the end of the road to park your car

## Walk directions

**1** You can't help but notice a very colourfully decorated toilet block at the car park before you set off on your walk, which begins at a large sign. Cross the dunes by veering slightly to the right to emerge at the mouth of Bream Creek, which flows into the sea here.

**2** Walk along the beach for about three kilometres to its end. Walking near the water's edge is not only easier on the legs but also less threatening to birds, which may be nesting near the dunes. They become very nervous if disturbed and will often desert their nest with dire consequences.

**3** From the end of the spit, across Marion Narrows, you will be able to see Little Chinaman Bay on the far north-western tip of the Forestier Peninsula and a small navigation light. Boats may be passing by on their way to or from the Denison Canal at Dunalley which is to the south-west. Looking

## Tasmanian history – Denison Canal

Denison Canal is 2.4 kilometres long and is located at Dunalley on the narrow isthmus which separates the Forestier and Tasman Peninsulas from the rest of Tasmania. It shortens the sea journey from the East Coast to Hobart by 80 kilometres and it is common for Sydney to Hobart yacht racers to use the canal as a convenient shortcut on their return voyage to Sydney. The canal is Australia's only purpose-built, hand-dug sea canal. Up to fifty men shovelled soil, clay, gravel and rock into railway wagons and from there into punts which took the material out to sea to be dumped. A swing bridge was installed for road traffic. It took three years to build and was completed and opened in 1905. In 1965 a new hydraulic swing bridge replaced the original bridge.

# 16 The Long Spit to Marion Bay

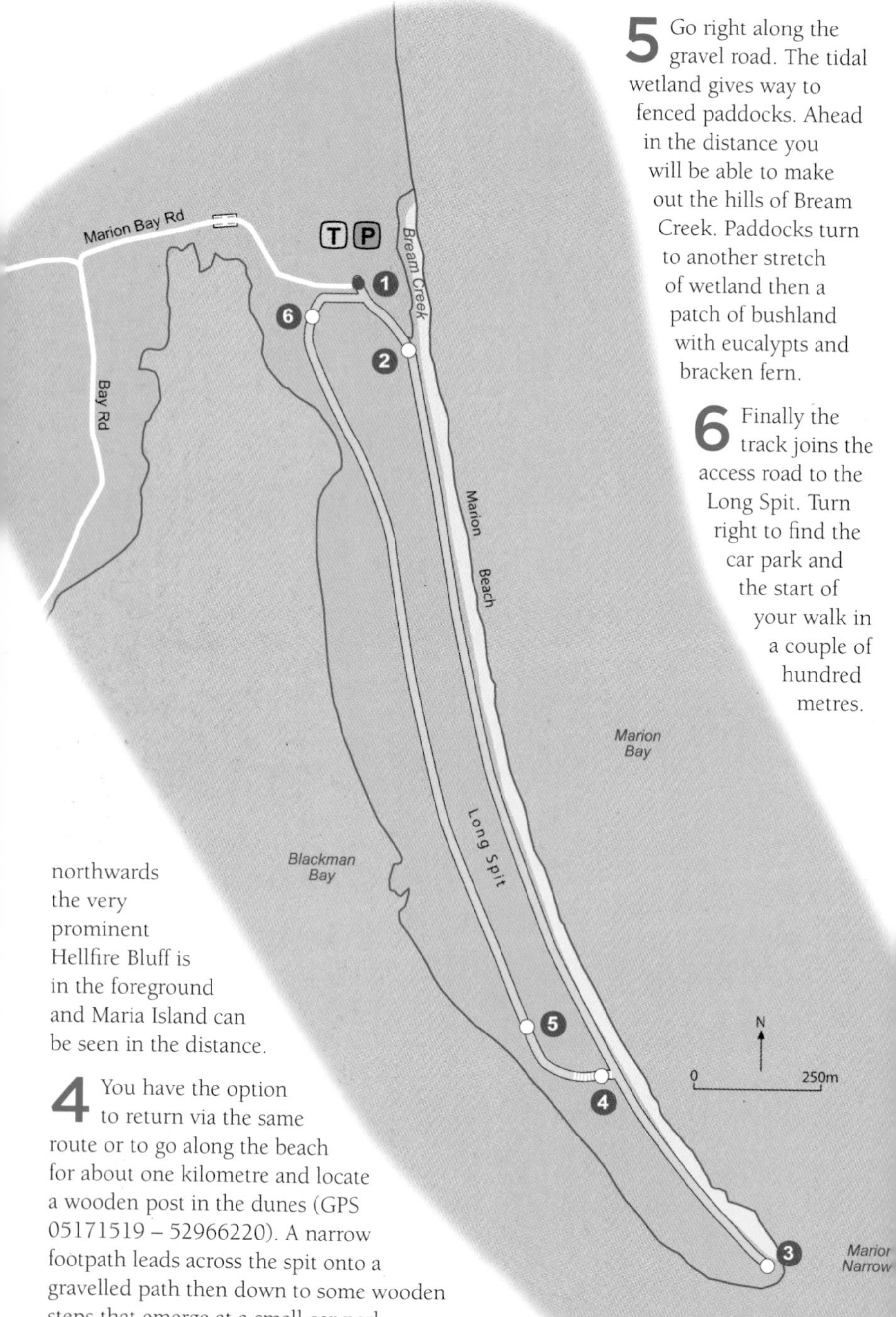

**5** Go right along the gravel road. The tidal wetland gives way to fenced paddocks. Ahead in the distance you will be able to make out the hills of Bream Creek. Paddocks turn to another stretch of wetland then a patch of bushland with eucalypts and bracken fern.

**6** Finally the track joins the access road to the Long Spit. Turn right to find the car park and the start of your walk in a couple of hundred metres.

Marion Bay Rd

Bay Rd

Bream Creek

Marion Beach

Marion Bay

Long Spit

Blackman Bay

Marion Narrow

**1**
**2**
**3**
**4**
**5**
**6**

N

0          250m

northwards the very prominent Hellfire Bluff is in the foreground and Maria Island can be seen in the distance.

**4** You have the option to return via the same route or to go along the beach for about one kilometre and locate a wooden post in the dunes (GPS 05171519 – 52966220). A narrow footpath leads across the spit onto a gravelled path then down to some wooden steps that emerge at a small car park.

## Tasmanian history – Tasman Monument

About three kilometres east from the end of the spit, on the fairly inaccessible Cape Paul Lamanon, stands the historically important Tasman Monument.

A concrete pillar erected by the Royal Society of Tasmania carries a plaque with the following inscription:

*At this spot the expedition under*

**Abel Jansz Tasman**

*being the first white people*

*to set foot on Tasmanian soil*

*planted the Dutch Flag on December 3rd 1642*

*as a memorial to the inhabitants of this country.*

*This stone was erected by the Royal Society of Tasmania 1923*

# Tasman Peninsula

The Tasman National Park was created in 1999 for its high scenic, cultural and natural conservation value. It occupies most of the coastline of the iconic Forestier and Tasman Peninsulas and several offshore islands such as Fossil Island, Hippolyte Rock and Tasman Island. The park contains some of the most stunning coastal scenery in Australia with dolerite sea cliffs ranging in height from 100 to 300 metres and spectacular rock formations that include sea caves, stacks, arches and collapse features created by the powerful wave action of recent millennia. The north-western corner of the Tasman Peninsula has some of the finest coastal sandstone exposures in Tasmania and contains the Coal Mines historic site which tells the story of early convict hardships. You will visit some of these iconic natural wonders and cultural features during the following walks.

Eaglehawk Neck

# 17 Devils Kitchen to Waterfall Bluff

The Tasman Peninsula was once a bleak place, chosen by Governor Arthur to accommodate a penal settlement. It is joined to the Forestier Peninsula to its north by a narrow isthmus known as Eaglehawk Neck. Today, coastal areas along the eastern side of the Forestier and Tasman Peninsulas and some southern and western areas of the Tasman Peninsula form the Tasman National Park. It contains some truly stunning coastal scenery, and is also home to a wide range of animals and plants, some of which are rare and not found elsewhere. This walk introduces you to just some of these wonderful features

## At a glance

**Grade:** Medium

**Time:** Total 3 hrs 15 mins return (1 hr 30 mins return from Devils Kitchen to Waterfall Bay; 1 hr 45 mins return from Waterfall Bay to Waterfall Bluff)

**Distance:** 6.75 km return

**Ascent/Descent:** 90 m/90 m

**Conditions:** The section from Devils Kitchen to Waterfall Bay is on a wide, gravelled, securely fenced path with slight undulations. The bush track from Waterfall Bay to Waterfall Bluff is narrow and steep but well-trodden, with unfenced, exposed cliff tops not suitable for children. Both sections are partly shaded

**Further information:** Parks and Wildlife Seven Mile Beach, T (03) 6214 8100 (Mon-Fri 0900-1645), www.parks.tas.gov.au

**Getting there**

**Car:** From Hobart take the Tasman Highway to Sorell then turn right into the Arthur Highway (A9) to the Tasman Peninsula. After passing Eaglehawk Neck and Pirates Bay to your left, turn left at the Blowhole, Tasmans Arch and Devils Kitchen sign and follow signage to Devils Kitchen. Park in the designated car park

# Walk directions

**1** The track begins at the *Patersons Arch 1 hr return, Waterfall Bay 2 hrs return* sign at the southern end of the car park and heads straight towards Waterfull Bluff which is visible from the start. It leads through coastal scrub which contains banksias, a low-growing necklace she-oak, tea-tree and swamp melaleuca, which sports showy, fluffy mauve flowers in spring.

Melaleuca

Bauera

**2** After about five minutes you will reach a lookout which allows you to see the 100-metre high sea cliffs back along the rugged coastline to the north.

**3** A further five minutes brings you to another lookout with an interpretive panel telling you about the interactions of life forms in the sea. From here the track begins to climb gradually through wet forest with the dainty pink-flowered baueras, melaleucas and banksias in the understorey. There are many other botanical delights to be found here, including trigger plants, stinkwood and native daphne. This area also supports rich birdlife and you may hear cockatoos and honeyeaters overhead.

**4** Shortly you will reach a third lookout towards the spectacular Patersons Arch.

**5** The next viewing platform, not much further along, allows you to look south, with Hippolyte Rocks and Cape Hauy in the distance. You will notice tall shrubs such as native hop bush, blanket bush and wild cherry growing along the track as you make your way to a platform which gives you a particularly good view back along the coast.

**6** The last lookout along this first section of the track gives a spectacular view into Waterfall Bay, with the waterfall clearly visible across the small bay, especially after rain. Directly after this you will reach a locked boom gate to mark the end of this easy part of your walk.

**7** There are two more lookouts at the Waterfall Bay car park which is at the end of Waterfall Bay Road. Here you have the option to turn back and retrace your steps to your car.

**8** Otherwise continue diagonally across the car park towards the *Tasman Coastal Track* sign and enter the narrow bush track which rises steeply into the tall stringy bark forest above. You will soon

Tasman Blowhole

Blowhole Rd

Doo Town

Tasman Arch Rd

TASMAN ARCH STATE RESERVE

Tasman Arch

**1**

**2**

**3**  Devils Kitchen

Blowhole Creek

Waterfall Bay Rd

N

0        500m

**4**  Paterson Arch

**5**

**6**

**7** P

Tasman Coastal Track

**8**

Waterfall Bay

FORTESCUE FOREST RESERVE

**9**

**11**

**12**  Waterfall Bluff

**10**

Tasman Trail

see a walker registration box where you can register your walk. The track leads up to the top of the cliffs of Waterfall Bay and to the top of the waterfall you saw from the lookout. After about ten minutes of climbing, as the track draws closer to the unfenced cliffs, you will be able to catch glimpses back down to Waterfall Bay.

**9** In about fifteen minutes the track begins to dip down slightly and you will note an unfenced rocky area on your left where (if you don't suffer from fear of heights) you can carefully stare into the incredible abyss!

**10** Next you will note a patch of tall cutting grass which indicates that you are

Shower Falls

traversing a wet spot where several small watercourses are heading for the cliff. Soon afterwards you will reach Camp Falls, a delightful small waterfall below a small bush camp. A wooden footbridge crosses the creek, above the falls, to a signposted track junction with the Waterfall Bluff track. Keep left to follow it along the cliff top.

**11** Keep left and after about 20 metres from the wooden sign you will note a fainter footpath leading off to the left along the top of the creek bank. Follow it for a few minutes as it descends down the man fern-filled watercourse to Shower Falls. You can actually walk behind these falls.

**12** Return to the main track and in only a couple of minutes you will reach an area from where you can see all of Waterfall Bay with Pirates Bay in the background, then after a few more minutes you can catch another stunning view of this iconic coastline. Take care to not lose your footing, particularly in high winds. The track continues in a southerly direction from here. Turn back at this point and retrace your walk back to your starting point. You are bound to notice things along the way that you missed on your way up.

Waterfall Bay

# 17 Devils Kitchen to Waterfall Bluff

Tasmans Arch

Blowhole

## Make a day of it – The Tasman Peninsula

The Tasman Peninsula is one of Tasmania's most visited areas, full of natural and historic features. You may wish to add a few of the following side trips to your walk.

From the Arthur Highway you can take a left turn at the top of a rise before Eaglehawk Neck, signed *Pirates Beach Lookout.* This is a 4 km loop road that rejoins the Arthur Highway just before Eaglehawk Neck. You can see 'the Neck' and all of Pirates Beach with Waterfall Bluff and Clemes Peak in the background from the car park at the lookout. The road continues down towards another car park from where a ten minute stroll along a wide gravel path will lead you to the famous **Tesselated Pavement**, a unique rock platform.

A little further along you can park your car and visit the quaint **Officers Quarters Museum** and perhaps take the short walk to the narrowest part in 'the Neck' where a bronze sculpture immortalises the infamous dog line that was installed from shore to shore to prevent convicts from escaping.

As you drive along the Tasmans Arch Road you will pass through **Doo Town**, which was originally a holiday shack-town. Each shack was given a name that included the word Doo. Look out for these amusing names.

**Tasmans Arch** and **Devils Kitchen** are situated near the start of this walk and are well worth a quick visit.

The **Blowhole** is a one-kilometre detour from Tasmans Arch Road and is well signposted. A van in the large car park there sells takeaway food and there are public toilets nearby. You can reach the Blowhole and a well-fenced lookout across Fossil Bay via short tracks.

# 18 Cape Hauy

Named for the well-known French mineralogist Rene-Juste Hauy, the Cape sports a group of spectacular sea stacks with intriguing names, such as the Monument, the Candlestick and the Totem Pole which are the main features of this most enjoyable walk. The track has been upgraded recently to form part of the planned Three Capes Walk which will showcase the magnificent coastal scenery of the Tasman Peninsula.

View from Cape Hauy Track

## At a glance

**Grade:** Medium

**Time:** 5 hrs

**Distance:** 10.5 km return

**Ascent/Descent:** 186 m/186 m

**Conditions:** Recently rebuilt wide foot track with stone steps in steep sections. Exposed section near Cape Hauy. Unfenced cliff edges. Parks passes apply

**Further information:** Parks and Wildlife Seven Mile Beach, T (03) 6214 8100 (Mon- Fri 0900-1645), www.parks.tas.gov.au

**Getting there**

**Car:** Take the Arthur Highway (A9) towards Port Arthur. About 4 kilometres south of the Tasmanian Devil Park at Taranna turn left into road signed Fortescue Bay and follow it to the day visitor car park at its end

## Walk directions

**1** The start of the track is signed and leads along the rocky foreshore to a boat ramp and camp area.

**2** Continue along the shore past another sign informing you that it is four hours return to Cape Hauy. The track initially follows the coast as it rises through eucalypt forest with an understorey of blanket bush, dolly bush and prickly box. Some friendly Bennett's wallabies roam this area. As you gain height you will be able to get clear views of Fortescue Bay on your left and if you are in luck you may be able to spot whales or dolphins that often visit this area.

**3** A steepish climb up some well-built steps leads to the top of the first knoll from where the track veers right and slopes down gently to cross a minor watercourse via a beautifully built stone arch, then up by a long stone 'stairway'. You may be able to spot native fuchsia and rice flower here.

**4** You will pass a small wet area which is indicated by the large tufts of cutting grass that grow here. You may also have noticed the endemic Oyster Bay pines. The Peninsula is home to a diverse flora and depending on the time of year you may be able to find flowering trigger plants, guitar plants, heath and orchids along the track as well. Wherever there is rich plant life, birds and animals will be found to avail themselves of the food source. You can expect to hear and see honeyeaters, fairy-wrens, scarlet robins, and pardalotes.

**5** If you happen to spot a Y-junction (which is part of the old track), keep

Climbing blueberry
(*Billardiera longiflora*)

left. More steep climbing will be followed by a level section, partly duckboarded, to help you get your breath back. You will pass a small swampy area where you can see the nodding flowers of the native dog rose, coral fern and of course cutting grass again, because it likes the wet spots.

**6** A couple more minor ups and downs and you will reach the junction with the track to Mount Fortescue and Cape Pillar which forms part of the Three Capes Walk mentioned in the introduction. At 186 metres, this is the highest point of the track and also about halfway to Cape Hauy. Keep left and soon you will get your first glimpse of the Cape.

**7** Shortly you will come to a bedrock area from where, on a clear day, you will be able to see the sea stacks off the Cape known as the Candlestick, Mitre Rock and The Lantern and further away the little island beyond known as the Hippolytes. This is also a traditional bushwalkers' resting spot either on the way to or on the way back from the Cape.

**8** The track begins to dip down steeply to cross an open saddle then up again for the last steep climb. Expansive views to north, east and south can be enjoyed in this exposed area, where plants are wind-pruned and stunted by salty air.

**9** You will pass a large subsidence

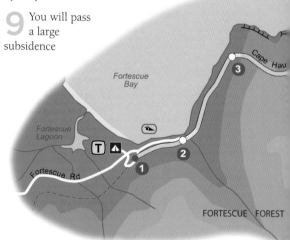

hole on your left as the Cape narrows. Directly the track skirts around the left side of the cape before you come to the end of the track. Take care not to get too close to the edge of the sea cliffs; the safest way to look down is lying on your stomach! Enjoy the views, to the north along the coast of the Tasman and Forestier Peninsulas, Maria Island and as far as Schouten Island south of Freycinet

View to Cape Pillar from Cape Hauy Track

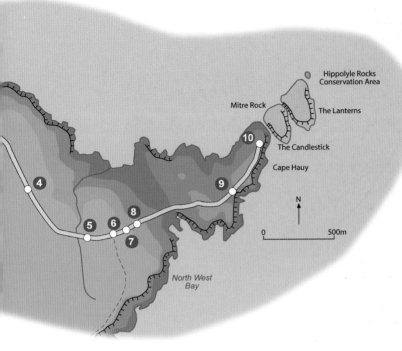

Hippolyte Rocks
Conservation Area

Mitre Rock

The Lanterns

**10**

The Candlestick

Cape Hauy

**4**

**9**

**8**

**5** **6**

**7**

N

0        500m

North West
Bay

Peninsula. North-east is Hippolyte rocks where seals are known to breed. The Cape to the south is Cape Pillar with Tasman Island beyond.

**10** Perhaps it is time to enjoy a meal and stay a while before returning to your start point via the same route. As you return, look for echidnas which can often be found fossicking for ants among the rocks. Many lizards also inhabit this area so it is worth taking your time.

## Tasmanian fauna – Echidna or Spiny Anteater (*Tachyglossus aculeatus*)

The Tasmanian echidna has more fur and less spines than mainland forms. It can weigh up to four kilograms. It is an egg-laying mammal known as monotreme (its only relative is the platypus). The eggs are soft shelled and the young hatch in about ten days and are suckled for three months before they are weaned. The echidna has poor eyesight and if you keep still when encountering one of these little fellows, you can observe it at very close range (echidnas have been known to climb over the top of people's boots!). It forages for ants, termites and other small invertebrates which it traps with its long sticky tongue.

## Tasmanian environment – The Totem Pole

This single, freestanding dolerite pillar, dwarfed by the larger Candlestick formation next to it, measures only four metres across the base and is over 60 metres tall. It can sway in high winds and tremble as waves pound its base. Rock climbers are attracted to it as it is said to be one of the most difficult vertical climbs in Australia. It was first climbed by Tim Christie in 1965 who also named it.

Cape Hauy Track

# 19 Crescent Bay and Mount Brown

Heath-covered sand dunes, rocky platforms, expansive coastal views, a mountain climb and a secluded beach are featured in this walk which begins at Remarkable Cave, one of the many popular tourist attractions on the Tasman Peninsula.

Crescent Beach

## At a glance

**Grade:** Medium

**Time:** 4 hrs 30 mins

**Distance:** 9.5 km return

**Ascent/Descent:** 173 m/173 m

**Conditions:** Exposed, partly sandy, very rocky ascent to Mount Brown trig; descent can be treacherous in wet weather

**Further information:** Parks and Wildlife Seven Mile Beach, T (03) 6214 8100 (Mon-Fri 0900-1645), www.parks.tas.gov.au

**Getting there**

**Car:** Take the Arthur Highway (A9) to Port Arthur. About 500 metres past Port Arthur turn left into Safety Cove Road (C347) which leads to Remarkable Cave, and park car at the end of the road

## Walk directions

**1** From Remarkable Cave car park walk back up the road about 100 metres to the entrance to the track, signed *Crescent Bay 4 hrs return, Mount Brown 4 hrs return*. Initially the track rises to the crest of a dune through a beautiful variety of coastal heath which includes rice flower, daisy bush, wild fuchsia, tea-tree, prickly mimosa and banksia. In spring you can expect to see many of them flowering.

**2** Once you reach the crest of the dune you will gain views back to Remarkable Cave and Cape Raoul in the distance. The vegetation is low due to constant wind and salt pruning and many of the shrubs have taken on the appearance of bonsais. Take care not to trip over their roots as these tend to jut into the sandy track in places. As you descend into swales the vegetation is taller due to the shelter and extra moisture there.

**3** After about fifteen minutes you will pass a sand blow on top of a dune which serves as a fine lookout.

**4** About ten minutes later a large area of bedrock, covered in patches of bright yellow lichen, comes into view on your right. A big rock cairn has been erected here, however you have to leave the track briefly to inspect this feature.

**5** Continue along the track to the next point of interest: the Maingon Blowhole. Keep well away from its crumbly, unstable

Remarkable Cave

## Tasmanian environment – Remarkable Cave

On your return from Crescent Bay you may have the time and inclination to inspect Remarkable Cave. It is only a 300-metre return walk down some well-built steps. There is some excellent, easy to understand and well-illustrated interpretation about this 'remarkable' erosion feature at the Maingon Bay Lookout, near the car park, which will help you to 'read the rocks' down at the cave's viewing platform.

edge as you skirt past it towards another bedrock area. Cross this parallel to the coast (ignoring any yellow tapes that lead inland). The track is a little overgrown here and you may have to push through the prickly vegetation.

**6** The track snakes through another sand blow. Go straight ahead

cairn, which marks the side track to the summit of Mount Brown, go right. The ascent is mostly over bare rock and zigzags steeply upwards with rock cairns showing the way. Lots of lizards call this area

home. Magnificent views across Crescent Bay are gained as you climb higher and higher.

**8** Soon a large cairn, more like a pile of rocks, will appear ahead. It is another five minutes from here to the summit where you will find a trig. Make a note of the track you arrived on for your return, as the flat

ignoring a very minor side track. The track now swings left, and the 'bonsai' shrubs you will find here include banksia, low-growing necklace she-oak, common fringe myrtle and rice flower.

**7** When you reach a junction and a small

Safety Cove

To Port Arthur

Safety Cove Rd

Dog Bark Rd

Briggs Point

P 1 2

Remarkable Cave

3

Basket Bay

POINT PUER CRESCENT BAY STATE RESERVE

10

4

5

Standu Point

Maingon Blowhole

N

0   500m

Crescent Bay

6

11

7

8

9

Mount Brown

Dauntless Point

summit plateau is crisscrossed with informal tracks.

9 From the trig you will be able to see most of the eastern coastline of the Tasman Peninsula which includes Cape Pillar and the steep cliffs of Tasman Island with its lighthouse. Having drunk in the spectacular scenery, descend back to the track junction at the base of Mount Brown and turn right to visit Crescent Bay. After a steep dip on the sandy track through some dense coastal vegetation you finally plunge down a large dune to the beach.

Crescent Beach

10 As you walk you will come across an area of odd-looking, spiky bedrock about halfway along the beach.

A very simple explanation is that this was formed when local mudstone was cooked and hardened by a Jurassic dolerite intrusion beneath it. Mineral-laden water subsequently passed through cooling cracks in the mudstone depositing iron oxides which resisted weathering and were therefore left standing proud of the cooked mudstone, which is what you see today. The top of the dolerite intrusion can be found at low tide level.

11 Having enjoyed a break, return to the start point, going straight ahead where the summit track to Mount Brown joins (unless you want to climb the lofty height twice!).

Trig on Mt Brown summit

Although this walk is described as a circuit of medium grade, you have the option of undertaking it as an easy grade return walk, with Lagoon Beach as your destination (recommended for children). To allow for this option, the circuit is described in a clockwise fashion. The full circuit, which leads around the base of Black Rock Hill is for experienced walkers. They will be rewarded with fantastic formations along the Triassic sandstone shelves of Green Head — so named for the shallow, clear, turquoise-coloured seawater lapping its shores. You will pass an extinct volcano of tertiary origin which has spewed bubbly black lava into the sea and conclude the walk with a sparsely taped route through bushland.

## At a glance

**Grade:** Hard for circuit/Easy for return

**Time:** 3 hrs 30 mins for circuit/2 hrs for return

**Distance:** 8.5 km for circuit/5.6 km for return

**Ascent/Descent:** 185 m for circuit/ none for return

**Conditions:** Track to Lagoon Beach is level. Soft and sandy underfoot, beneath canopy of trees, remainder of track is a combination of rocky shore, cliff top and bush track. Two hours either side of low tide is best for the full circuit walk

**Further information:** Parks and Wildlife Seven Mile Beach, T (03) 6214 8100 (Mon-Fri 0900-1645), www.parks.tas.gov.au

**Getting there**

**Car:** From the Arthur Highway (A9) turn right into B37, just south of the Tasmanian Devil Park at Taranna. At Premaydena turn right into Saltwater River Road (C341) and after 9.5 kilometres turn right into Lime Bay and Coalmines Road. The bitumen ends at the Coal Mines Historic Site (see below). Continue for another 2.5 kilometres to Lime Bay Camping Area and park at its far (north-western) end

## Walk directions

**1** Locate the fire trail at the north-western end of campground by a large sign informing about shore birds at Lagoon Beach and two white steel posts. It leads along a dune behind Lagoon Beach then swings left and rises gently into bushland with peppermint gums dominating overhead and an understorey of bracken fern and saggs.

**2** In a short while the vegetation becomes more interesting with wattles, banksias and native cherry trees joining the gums, together with an array of wildflowers, particularly during spring and summer. The sandy soil supports many small orchids which can be found by those with a keen eye. After about twenty minutes you will be able to catch glimpses of Sloping Lagoon through the trees on your left and ten minutes later, after going through a patch of tea-tree (two species, *Leptospermum scoparium* with small shiny leaves and *L. lanigerum* with silvery leaves), you will approach a large dune on the far side of the lagoon.

**3** Continue to follow the main trail, ignoring any narrow foot tracks on either

Clematis aristata

side and a wider track which joins from the left after about one hour.

**4** Directly after passing this wider track, a tall dune will appear. The track winds along and then across the dune in order to reach Lagoon Beach behind it. You will hear the ocean ahead and once you crest the dune you are rewarded

with expansive views across Fredrick Henry Bay to Sloping Island and beyond to Bruny Island on the left and the South Arm Peninsula on the right.

**5** Turn right to walk along the waterline of the beach to avoid inadvertently stepping onto nests of shorebirds which congregate in this area in large numbers. The far end of the beach is contained by a beautiful, small sandstone headland.

**6** At this point you have the option to return to the start point of this walk. Otherwise, to continue the circuit, locate the steep narrow track to your right, marked by a pink ribbon at the top, which leads up between the sandstone and the dune. A slightly awkward scramble will get you to the top of the headland.

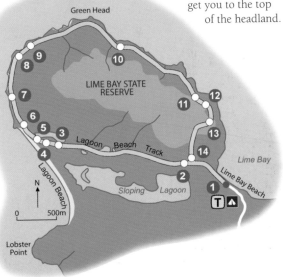

The taped route leads back down to the waterline where the clear, turquoise waters of the bay lap the colourful sandstone.

**7** At low tide you can amble along the beautifully layered sandstone shelving of the rocky shore, admire nature's sculptural works, watch shore birds and find interesting shells.

**8** Where the shore becomes impassable at the next small headland it is a short, easy scramble up the bank to the taped route which is visible from below.

**9** Continue to follow the route which leads along the cliff tops beneath she-oaks. The tapes are at times difficult to locate, so keep within sight of the coast and follow the path of least resistance. Some spots along the way allow you to marvel at the wafer-thin sandstone overhangs (and why it would be a bad idea to stand on top of them!). You may also notice that some huge blocks of sandstone have fallen into the sea.

**10** On the way from Green Head to Lime Bay the track zigzags down to cross a steep-sided gully and there is a fine view down to a tiny beach from the other side. You will skirt around the top of three more watercourses as you contour around the steep base of Black Rock Hill.

**11** As the hill on your right begins to flatten you will pass some large

Lagoon Beach

## Tasmanian flora – Waxlip orchid (*Glossodia major*)

This attractive orchid is widespread in sandy areas of dry woodlands and heathlands. Its flower, mostly about 4 centimetres in diameter, grows on slender, hairy stems to a height of about 25 centimetres. Flowers come in shades of blue to mauve, rarely white. They are often the first of the orchids to be found flowering in spring.

blue gums and a small rock cairn, made of black bubbly lava, sitting on a boulder indicating that this area was volcanic. You may have also observed some small, old lava flows down to the coast along the way.

**12** You will cross a couple of areas with lots of dead sticks and logs serving as lookouts towards Primrose Sands and Dunnally on the Tasmanian mainland. Just when you may be finding it a bit tiresome to look for the track markers, Lime Bay Beach will come into view up ahead.

**13** Alas, the track veers right and you quickly lose sight of the beach as the track leads uphill through tall bracken fern. You can see Black Rock Hill to your right through the open forest as you reach a crest from where you will be able to glimpse Sloping Lagoon. Veer slightly to the left and take the now more visible track downhill through head-high tea-tree scrub until it joins the main track you walked earlier.

**14** Go left and you will reach your start point in about five minutes.

## Tasmanian environment – Triassic sandstone

The South Pole was somewhere near the present day town of Bourke in NSW during some of the Triassic. Plants and animals would have had to live with several months of darkness, and the midnight sun for the rest of the time. The dominant plants were Dicroidium seed ferns. It was before and near the beginning of the Triassic that the first mammal-like reptiles, the Cynodonts, appeared. They evolved into mammals during this time. The supercontinent Pangaea began to break into Laurasia and Gondwana towards the end of the Triassic which preceded the Jurassic when the final break occurred. Geologists can read these and other stories in the rocks. The northern end of the Tasman Peninsula has some of the finest exposures of Triassic sandstone south of Sydney, rivalling those of the Painted Cliffs at Maria Island. The coloured, sedimentary layers tell the story of changing climates and life forms on earth at the time they were deposited.

# 21 Clark Cliffs

You can spend a pleasant three hours on this bushwalk where the emphasis is definitely on the bush. Managed by Forestry Tasmania, this is an area of tall trees with a rich understorey of wet forest species. Birds love this kind of habitat and you will hear and see many of them. In autumn you will also delight in the large array of fungi to be found. Twice during the walk you will be rewarded, weather permitting, with wide views across the peninsula and out to sea: once to Norfolk Bay to the north and again from your destination towards the south-west of the Tasman Peninsula.

## At a glance

**Grade:** Medium

**Time:** 3 hrs

**Distance:** 7.4 km return

**Ascent/Descent:** 160 m/160 m

**Conditions:** Shady 4WD track, then taped route (care needs to be taken to follow tapes/markers); a steady, not very steep climb

### Getting there

**Car:** From the Arthur Highway (A9) turn right into B37, just south of the Tasmanian Devil Park at Taranna. After 4.4 kilometres turn left into Fire Tower Rd. Drive 5.4 kilometres and park car in small area on right at the start of the walk signposted *Clark Cliffs via Lookout*

Coral fungus (Clavaria sp.)

## Walk directions

**1** Set off on the disused, gently rising 4WD track in a northerly direction. The track is carpeted with moss and leaf litter and is lined with an understorey of dogwood, Tasmanian blanket leaf, cutting grass and other wet forest species that occasionally overhang the track.

**2** After about ten minutes you will find the first fallen tree that needs to be detoured around. Passing a lower lying area you will see some manferns and berry bushes. There are colourful fungi to be found among the moss-covered rocks along the track as well.

**3** As you gain height, the track begins to curve to the left (NW)

Armillaria fungus

and you will reach a sign pointing to Norfolk Bay Lookout on the right. It is only a one-minute detour towards two tall gums and a small sign informing you that you have reached an elevation of 427 metres.

The lookout is furnished with a lovingly built stone seat on the edge of sheer dolerite columns from where you can overlook the farmland around Koonya and see across to Norfolk Bay and the Forestier Peninsula.

**4** Return to the main track; pass under a large log that has fallen across the track to a *Clark Cliffs* sign, directing you to the left.

**5** From here on you will be walking in a southerly direction following a taped route with orange tape and markers. The path turns into a bit of an obstacle course with fallen sticks and logs to be negotiated. You will be climbing steadily most of the way. Some interesting plants such as dragon heath,

Plummers Creek

Mount Clark

Musk Forest

Clark Cliffs

N

0          200m

Fire Tower Rd

native laurel and mountain correa grow in this area.

**6** Shortly you will cross the headwaters of Plummers Creek where you will find a fine stand of manferns, very tall gum trees and the inevitable cutting grass. Perhaps you will hear the melodious song of the mountain jay in the canopy above.

**7** After another steady climb past the summit of Mount Clark (494 metres) you will reach the edge of Clark Cliffs which begin here. A sign directs you to the right where a one-minute walk will take you to a wonderful view down to a magnificent musk forest.

**8** Go back to the main track and climb over the trash from a large fallen dead tree. From here it is only a short, gentle downhill walk to the *Clarks Cliff* sign and the information that you are now 480 metres above sea

Clark Cliffs

## Tasmanian flora – Cutting grass (*Gahnia grandis*)

Whenever you see this grand, very tall, structural grass-like plant you can be certain that it is going to be wet underfoot, regardless of whether you are at sea level or on top of a mountain. The plant should probably be nicknamed 'Tripping Grass' as it tends to get hold of your boots causing you to trip. The rough leaves grow up to 1.5 metres long, and have razor-sharp, serrated edges; it's not a plant to hang onto and definitely not child-friendly. Cutting grass flowers in late spring and summer with flower heads reaching a height of up to 3.5 metres.

level. The best views are from a few metres further down the track from the position of the signs. On a clear day the south-west of the Tasman Peninsula makes for a great panorama to enjoy.

**9** Make your way back to the start point when you are ready. The return walk is likely to take less time, particularly once you have reached the 4WD track.

### Tasmanian flora – Musk (*Olearia argophylla*)

Musk is a common tall shrub or small tree in shady, wet forests which can grow to 15 metres tall. The large oval leaves are light green with a hairy, silvery underside and coarsely toothed margins. The daisy-like, creamy-white flower clusters appear in early summer. Timber from this attractive plant was once prized by cabinetmakers particularly for inlay work. While the grain of the wood is mainly straight, burls that often form near the base of the tree create beautiful, brown, swirly patterns.

# 22 Mount Stewart – Coal Mines Circuit

A visit to the low summit of this lesser-known hill allows commanding, tree-framed views of the north-western wing of the Tasman Peninsula and across Storm Bay to Cremorne and the Wellington Range. It can easily be combined with viewing some of the more prominent sites of the Coal Mines Historic Site near Premaydena, making it into a relaxed day's outing. Flora and birdlife are plentiful in the attractive, open bush areas along the way and the convict history is well interpreted to make for a most interesting and enjoyable walk.

## At a glance

**Grade:** Easy

**Time:** Walking time 2 hrs 15 mins, but allow much more for viewing historic sites.

**Distance:** 6.7 km circuit

**Ascent/Descent:** 122 m/122 m

**Conditions:** Sandy bush trails and tracks, minor ascent to rocky top of Mount Stewart for panoramic views

**Further information:** Parks and Wildlife Seven Mile Beach, T (03) 6214 8100 (Mon-Fri 0900-1645), www.parks.tas.gov.au

## Getting there

**Car:** From the Arthur Highway (A9) turn right into B37, just south of the Tasmanian Devil Park at Taranna. At Premaydena turn right into Saltwater River Road (C341) and after 9.5 kilometres turn right into Lime Bay and Coal Mine Road. The bitumen ends at the Coal Mines Historic Site. Drive past the site and turn left at the Air Shaft sign. Park car in small parking area

## Walk directions

**1** Take the sandy disused road to the left of the barred road which leads west and uphill through open bushland of black peppermint and white gum with bracken fern in the understorey and some handsome native cherry trees. In a couple of minutes, views down to Sloping Main Beach appear as you crest a small rise. The understorey becomes more interesting with heath plants ranging in colour from white to red and the low-growing necklace she-oak.

**2** Before you turn right at the next junction, you can inspect the historic Air Shaft which you will see, fully fenced, up ahead. After the right turn the track leads uphill for a short distance giving you a view to the south-east out to sea.

**3** You will cross a low spot with tea-tree and scented paperbark with its creamy coloured bottlebrush flowers. Ignore a side track and shortly you will reach a T-junction with a fire trail.

**4** Turn left and after about 30 metres veer right into an overgrown bush track which gradually curves right in a north-easterly direction to climb the summit of Mount

Stewart. The banksias here attract parrots, wattlebirds and other honeyeaters which can be heard in the canopy above. As you gain height, the track steepens, the bush becomes drier and the ground rockier. Black wattle dominates and there is evidence that this area was once used as a bush grazing block.

**5** The rocky summit is reached shortly as you walk by a pile of brick rubble and barely discernable foundations of a former semaphore station. To get the full benefit of the views, you can treat yourself to a little wander around the sparsely vegetated summit which is actually the eroded core of a volcano from Tertiary times (only about 15 million years ago).

**6** Return to the sandy fire trail and turn left to follow it east in a straight line towards the coast.

**7** When you reach the main access road, which leads through the site, turn right and carefully cross it to continue straight ahead along the Old Mine Road, signposted *Incline*, which leads to a small car park and a barred gate.

**8** Pass the gate, and a few steps along you will see the access track to view the Incline. You may wish to inspect this, then return to the main trail and

take the narrow foot track to Plunkett Point which heads east and downhill along the former incline through a patch of tea-tree to the former jetty site.

**9** In only a few minutes you will emerge at the coast. There is much to see here including an intriguing 'viewing device'. This may be a good spot to rest as well.

**10** Continue your walk by turning right into the bush track which leads uphill along the coast. The ruins of the Officers Quarters can be looked over along the way before the track rejoins the Old Mine Road and the extensive ruins of the Convict Precinct come into view. After inspecting this gruesome site of much human misery, exit it at

Convict precinct

the top side in a north-easterly direction on the track marked *Military Precinct*. The track swings north past the scant ruins of the Superintendant's and Officers Quarters built of brick and sandstone overlooking picturesque Norfolk Bay and the convict precinct.

**11** The track now swings left to pass a former vegetable garden area, then right and uphill to climb to the top of Coal Mine Hill where little remains of a semaphore station that once relayed messages from Port Arthur to Hobart.

**12** From the station site go downhill through saggs, bracken fern and native cherries to the Main Mine Shaft which is well fenced and interpreted.

**13** Exit past a large boiler to reach a car park. Just below it, locate a foot track which initially runs parallel to the access road then veers right toward the Air Shaft car park and your start point, crossing the Main Access Road along the way.

## Tasmanian history – Coal Mines historic site

This site is of historical significance because it contains Tasmania's first operational mine. It was run to reduce reliance on imported, expensive coal from New South Wales. Convicts with the most serious convictions were employed in the mine as punishment between 1833 and 1848, after which time it operated for another 25 years.

Badajos Street, Ross

# Midlands Villages

Village walks in rural Tasmania offer a very special kind of relaxation. As you wander along streets lined with Georgian buildings and European trees, you will be transported back in time to learn about Tasmania's convict past and the wonderful achievements of the town's early farmers and settlers. There will be chances to visit quaint local museums, read informative interpretive panels, browse small country shops and perhaps linger a while for a coffee or a meal. It follows that the walk times suggested below do not include any of the above, so you'll have to add extra time to include your own special interests.

# 23 Ross

This walk takes in all that is essentially Ross, including expansive views across the plains to the Great Western Tiers, which form the picturesque backdrop to this thriving village. Situated on the wide, fertile plains of the Macquarie River, famous for their superfine Merino wool production, Ross is one of Australia's oldest towns. Its main buildings and bridge were erected by convicts during the 1830s using local sandstone. The town's most important, and most photographed feature, the bridge, was designed by the prolific colonial architect, John Lee Archer, and decorated with carvings by the talented convict stonemason, Daniel Herbert.

## At a glance

**Grade:** Easy

**Time:** 1 hr 30 mins

**Distance:** 4.4 km circuit

**Ascent/Descent:** 20 m

**Conditions:** Foot tracks and grassy road verges; some street crossings

**Further information:** www.heritagehighway.com.au

**Getting there**

**Car:** Take the Midland Hwy (1), also known as Heritage Highway, and turn off at Ross. Locate the car park and picnic area below the SE corner of the historic Ross Bridge to park your car

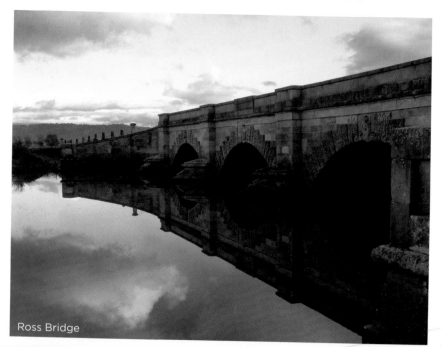

Ross Bridge

## Walk directions

**1** To begin your walk, exit through the gate behind the picnic hut and barbecue shelter to view the historic Old Stables which are built into the natural sandstone.

**2** Return to the bridge and Bridge Street, turn right taking care with incoming traffic. Pass a small playground and swimming pool. Across the street you can see the original barracks before you reach the main intersection of the town with its war memorial in the centre.

**3** An interesting feature of Ross is that at each corner of these crossroads is an important building said to represent an aspect of life. On your right, the south-western corner is 'Damnation' (gaol and police station, now a private residence), on your left, across the street on the north-western corner is 'Salvation' (the Catholic Church), the north-eastern corner represents 'Temptation' (Man O'Ross Hotel) and finally the south-eastern corner is 'Recreation' (the Town Hall). Turn right into Church Street, pass the Ross Memorial Building (c 1836) and the Tasmanian Wool Centre which is well worth a visit if you can spare the time (see box below).

Town Hall

## Out and about – Tasmanian Wool Centre

The centre was built in 1988 as a bicentennial project. It contains a heritage museum with graphic displays of the convict era, and military and grazing history as well as an excellent exhibit about wool production – from the sheep's back, to spinning, weaving and the finished garment. There are audiovisual displays on shearing technique and samples of superfine merino wool to touch and feel. A shop near the entrance stocks a wide range of woollen products including crafts (open Mon-Fri 0900-1700, Sat and Sun 0930-1700, entry is by donation).

**4** Further uphill, pass an old cottage, formerly an army headquarters, and the Drill Hall until you reach the prominent Uniting Church. It is built from local sandstone and its tall spire dominates the village.

**5** Continue uphill passing a small picnic table and lookout on the left. A sealed foot track with some steps leads downhill to the river flats from here. It is signed *Historic Walk* and ends at the Female Factory site.

**6** In about 200 metres you will see the Commandant's Cottage and walled enclosure of this historic site. You may wish to take some time to view the excellent interpretation panels within the site. Exit the site and continue eastwards to Bond Street.

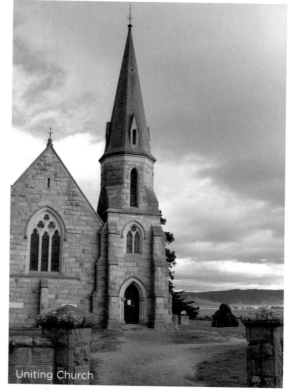

Uniting Church

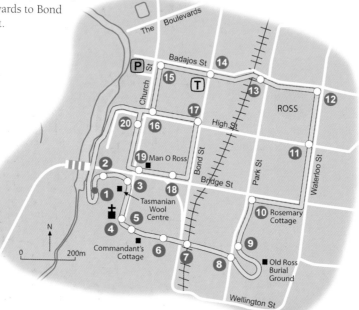

views back to the village, with the Great Western Tiers in the background on the horizon.

**9** Return to Park Street and turn right, passing the cemetery on the left and going downhill on the wide grassy road verge.

**10** Next turn right into Bridge Street, then left into Waterloo Street. Pass the charming Rosemary Cottage and St Johns Anglican cemetery on your right.

**11** Cross High Street. On the left is the local sports ground.

**12** Turn left into Badajos Street where you will pass some interesting chainsaw sculptures around a private residence.

**13** Recross the railway line and continue along the wide, now elm tree-lined street, which gives a colourful display in autumn. You will pass the charming Dray House

**7** Cross Bond Street and the railway line through the gates provided and walk on the gravelled path along the full length of a beautiful stone wall built out of cut stones, filled and capped with rubble. The wall forms the boundary of the cemetery.

**8** Carefully cross Park Street to the signed *Old Ross Burial Ground* where you can inspect some unusual gravestones carved by the same convict artists that created the carvings on the Ross Bridge. From this relatively high point there are lovely (private) and another historic cottage.

**14** Cross Bond Street to walk by Forget-me-not Cottage which dates back to 1840 before you reach St Johns Anglican Church on the corner of Badajos Street and Church Street.

**15** Turn left into the charming, tree-lined Church Street, Ross's main street and centre of activity. Pass the original Ross Bakery which takes pride in having operated from this site for a hundred years. They have a nice interpretive sign outside the shop and some tasty bakery food inside.

**16** Next turn left into High Street, past St Johns School, the historic Hudson Cottage (1850) and two conjoined cottages as well as the historic

Methodist Sunday School and Chapel, now in private hands.

**17** Turn right into Bond Street, then right again into Bridge Street where you will find a quaint establishment with café, tea house, gift shop and accommodation all combined. Opposite the street overlooking a walled playing field is the old State School building which is well worth a slight detour for a closer look.

**18** Continuing back along Bridge Street to the right, you will pass the rear of the Man O'Ross Hotel.

**19** Turn right to revisit Church Street from the southern end. Pass the front of the Hotel. Across the street are the Catholic Church, the local shop, the Ross Village Market and the

post office with a couple of old red phone boxes a little further along.

**20** Turn left and walk towards the river. This is also the entrance to the local caravan park and motel. As their entrance road curves to the left, keep straight ahead to continue along the grassy river bank where there are some inviting seats. Soon the bridge comes into view. Remain on the river reserve as the track enters a short tree-lined area before emerging at the end of a long stone wall on the left and the bridge on the right. The bridge has a set of curved stairs at each of its four corners and you can go down them to get a better view of the intriguing carvings.

Finally, carefully cross Bridge Street back to your start point.

Old State School building

Catholic Church

# 24 Oatlands Historic Village

Oats were never grown in commercial quantities in this area as one might be led to believe. Oatlands was originally named Great Lagoon, but was renamed by Governor Macquarie in honour of the country seat of his patron, the Duke of York, who had appointed Macquarie governor of NSW. Oatlands was one of four military outposts along the road from Hobart to Launceston. It was once intended that Oatlands, with its central location almost halfway between Hobart and Launceston, would become Tasmania's interior capital. It was the only regional town in Tasmania to have a supreme court. No doubt you will discover many more interesting facts as you travel back in time on this walk through history.

## At a glance

**Grade:** Easy

**Time:** 1 hr 15 mins

**Distance:** 4.3 km circuit

**Conditions:** Footpaths and some street crossings

**Further information:** www.heritagehighway.com.au

**Getting there**

**Car:** Take the Midland Hwy (A1) and turn off into the township. Drive along High Street to the northern end of town and turn right into the Esplanade. Park on left side of road near BBQ and toilets

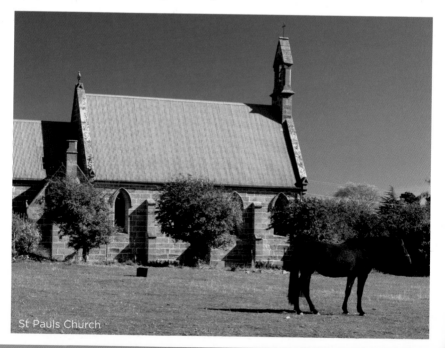

St Pauls Church

## Walk directions

**1** Locate a narrow lane, lined with stone walling that leads to the Callington Mill precinct. To your right you will find a café and tourist information room. The historic mill, which dates back to 1837 and has only very recently been fully restored, is on the left.

**2** Exit the precinct through a wooden gate into Mill Lane which leads onto High Street then go left. Pass the Midland Hotel then cross High Street towards a large historic wool press protected by a wooden shelter.

**3** Walk down the driveway of the stock and station agent past a small cottage on the right. The town's stock saleyards will appear in the distance below, not far from the Midland Highway bypass. The driveway leads onto a gravel road.

**4** Keep left to walk past the base of one of the many sandstone outcrops in the town and continue along the grassy track which curves left to join the bottom of South Parade Street.

**5** Continue along South Parade Street passing the rear of St Pauls Catholic Church which can be seen across a small paddock on your right.

**6** Turn right into Gay Street and, after viewing St Pauls, continue along Gay Street.

**7** Go left into William Street for a small side trip to see St Peters Anglican Church which will shortly come into view to your right. Enter the churchyard through an old stone gateway by a large oak tree for a closer look at the church and graveyard.

**8** Return to Gay Street and follow it until you reach High Street. You will pass the Rechabite Hall built by local stonemasons in the late 1800s.

**9** Go right at High Street. Across the street you will see the old State School building. Further along stands the Town Hall which was completed in 1881. A number of interesting shops can be browsed along the way before you pass the post office,

the Kentish Hotel and the former Roxy Theatre (now a supermarket) and sandstone bank building (c 1840) on the right and the district school on the left.

**10** After crossing Wellington Street you will reach the Casaveen Knitwear factory, showrooms and café which you may wish to inspect. Casaveen is a unique, local family business which has persisted through 22 years of market slumps and drought. Originally, local hand knitters were employed to produce custom-made garments from local wool. The knitters have been replaced by machines and factory tours are free.

**11** Further uphill along High Street stands the prominent Campbell Memorial Uniting Church originally built in 1856. Only two years later lightning struck the 30-metre tall steeple and destroyed the church, which was rebuilt later.

**12** Opposite the church on High Street are a playground, picnic table and local sports grounds. This may be a good spot to rest awhile before you return to Stanley Street and turn right. You will

notice that the footpath here is hewn from bedrock. A little further on the right you will see a cottage hugging a sandstone outcrop.

**13** Turn left into Marlborough Street and go towards Lake Dulverton where you will find a walking track which leads along its shore. A shallow sandstone basin underlies the lake which occupies over 200 hectares. In 1827 a dam was constructed by convicts to provide fresh water for the new settlement. Its remains

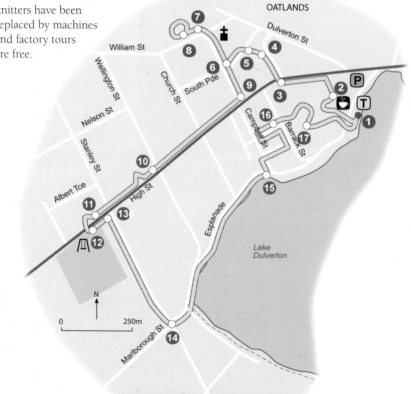

can still be seen behind the current concrete structure. A large proportion of this shallow lake is ephemeral (not permanent). This area is a haven for waterbirds and you can expect to see ducks, geese, swans, native hens and plovers among others.

**14** Go left along the shore past some

picnic tables with views to sandstone shelves across the lake. The tiny Mary Island can be seen on the right. It is accessible by foot in dry times and is part of the Lake Dulverton Conservation area. Pass a small outdoor exercise area.

**15** When you reach Campbell Street turn left. On the corner

stands the old courthouse (see below). Opposite is the local RSL Club which was built around the original watch house. Turn right into the very short Albert Street with two delightful cottages, then left into Barrack Street. The Mill will appear on your right.

**16** A small side trip to the left into Mason Street allows you to view the old gaol building with its worn stone steps, trodden by many feet. At the time of writing, an impressive stone archway which served as an entrance to the original State School building for many decades was in the process of being returned to the gaol site from where it had been 'borrowed'. Return to Barrack Street and go straight ahead towards the mill. The path leads across the former sheep sale yards area with some old post and rail fencing and stone wallling still visible. A small playground has been sited here in more recent times.

**17** Re-enter the Mill precinct and return to your start point.

Lake Dulverton

Old Gaol

## Walk variation

At waypoint 14 you have the option to extend your walk by turning right and walking along the shore of the lake. The track ends at the second bund wall which was constructed by volunteers in 1997 to create a separate water storage area during the long drought years in the 1990s and early 2000s. Water to fill this section of the dam was supplied from either a bore or piped from the Blackman River 17 kilometres north of Oatlands. Return to the end of Marlbrorough Street and continue along the lake shore as in waypoint 14.

## Sandstone – a close and handy building material

Oatlands claims to have the largest collection of original Georgian and Victorian sandstone buildings within a township in Australia. There are some 87 of them. Much of the sandstone was quarried from the shores of Lake Dulverton and many of the buildings were erected by convict labour.

The town's oldest building, the Courthouse, (cnr Campbell Street and Esplanade) was built in 1829 by two convicts from a chain gang who were wearing leg irons. A few years later, officer's quarters and a Commissariat's store and watch house were added, followed by the Gaol in 1835 and the Callington Mill. It has since been recycled as a chapel, council chambers and mechanics institute and from 1907 became a family home for 70 years.

## Tasmanian history – Callington Flour Mill

This is a Lincolnshire mill built by John Vincent in 1837. It was operated by various owners from 1837 to 1892 and is Australia's third oldest windmill. It was gutted by fire early last century and remained an empty shell for many decades. Bicentennial funding has allowed recent restoration of the milling mechanism by a British millwright who came especially to complete the task. It is now Australia's only working wind-powered flour mill in its original setting.

Historic Courthouse in Oatlands

# 25 Bothwell Highland Village

Bothwell lies on the banks of the Clyde River, which has shaped the fertile, broad plains that were once home to the Aboriginal Big River Tribe and which first attracted Scottish settlers to the area in 1823. Sheep, cattle and grain crops have been the bread and butter industries since white settlement. Bothwell boasts the first Aberdeen Angus cattle stud in Australia, the oldest golf course in the southern hemisphere and a whisky distillery, all as result of its Scottish heritage. This walk leads you past many of the town's historic buildings (there are 52 dating back to the early 1800s), including the famous golf museum. You will also cross the Clyde River and get a feel for the wide open spaces of the surrounding countryside from a vantage point on top of Adelaide (or Barrack) Hill.

## At a glance

**Grade:** Easy

**Time:** 1 hr

**Distance:** 2.1 km circuit

**Ascent/Descent:** 30 m

**Conditions:** Footpaths, walking tracks, some road crossings and a small climb. Exposed

**Further information:** www.discovertasmania.com/hobart_and_surrounds

**Getting there**

**Car:** From Hobart take the Midland Highway (A1) also known as the Heritage Highway and turn west at Melton Mowbray. Bothwell is only 21 kilometres away. Turn right into Market Place and park your car

## Walk directions

**1** The walk starts with Queens Park to your left, dotted with large deciduous trees, picnic tables and playgrounds. On your right are St Michaels and All Angels Church, the former school headmaster's residence, which is now the home of the Bothwell Historical Society and the old School House which more recently became the visitor information centre and golf museum. You may wish to visit the latter first before you embark on your walking tour, for further information on points of interest, historic attractions and services.

**2** To begin your walk, go to the northern end of Market Place, where you will find Bothwell's oldest church, St Lukes, built in 1830 to a design by the then government architect John Lee Archer who worked in this

capacity for eleven years (see box in Walk 26). You will encounter more of Archer's designs in Ross, Oatlands and Richmond. Turn left into Alexander Street, cross Queens Street and pass charming twin brick cottages on your left and the library on the right as you reach the Old Bothwell Store on the corner of Alexander and Dalrymple Street. The flagstones under your feet are original, over 140 years old, and would have many stories to tell! Across Dalrymple Street stands the Old Post Office building which dates back to 1891 and is now an antiques shop.

**3** Turn left into Dalrymple Street and shortly you will pass an imposing double-storey sandstone building which

was the Falls of Clyde Hotel, but is now in private hands.

**4** When you reach Patrick Street, which is the continuation of the Lake Highway, go right to follow the footpath that leads along an old wire fence with split posts and droppers. You are crossing the flood plains of the Clyde River. The road curves right and passes the local fire station. Carefully cross the highway towards the police station.

**5** Locate the entrance to Croakers Alley on the left, just past the station and enter it through the wooden gate (as a general rule, in the country, always leave gates as you find them, either open or shut to allow stock to move as the farmer intended). The old split post and rail fence on the right is a fine example of pre-wire fence building. Ahead, across the river, you can see the former Barracks perched on an outcrop of solid sandstone.

After rain you can hear a frog chorus as you walk along the grassy lane.

**6** Exit the lane through a steel gate towards a picnic table. Cross the river via a small wooden footbridge and go up the steps on the other side, then turn left into Wentworth Street. There are more picnic tables to the left, overlooking the river flats and village.

**7** Watch out for traffic as you turn right into Adelaide Street which leads uphill to the lookout. Take care crossing a cattle grid at the top and continue along the signed walking track which zigzags to the top of the hill where you will find an inviting seat and some boulders with a directional dial. Bothwell's water reservoirs are at the very top of the hill.

**8** After you have enjoyed the view, return to the grid and turn right just before the old dry stone wall. Walk along the wall until you reach a gate and a *Walking Track* sign.

**9** Turn left and walk downhill on the grassy track which has another stone wall on the right. The English hawthorn bushes here are so old, they have turned into trees. When you reach Wentworth Street again, you will note that this walking track is signposted as Lovers Lane.

**10** Go straight ahead along Logan Street which has a wide, grassy road verge and a hawthorn hedge on its right. Cross the bridge over the Clyde River and continue along Logan Street as it curves to the left, back toward the village centre.

**11** Keep right at a Y-junction to go up High Street where you will pass the quaint bootmakers shop on the right and another split post and rail fence. A small sheep

Old bootmaker's shop

## Tasmanian agriculture – Cattle

While the black Aberdeen Angus cattle are still dominant in the highlands around Bothwell, other breeds such as Murray Greys (a fixed breed derived from crossing Angus and Australian Shorthorn cattle) and Herefords are also common. The largest cattle sale conducted by a single stock agent is held annually at Bothwell. Buyers from all over Tasmania and Victoria are attracted to this sale as cattle bred in this high country are renowned for their vigour and ability to produce prime beef.

paddock and the back of the historic Castle Hotel can be seen across the street. Cross William Street which becomes the road to Ouse.

**12** Turn left into George Street which leads you back to Patrick Street (the highway to Melton Mowbray).

**13** Cross this carefully and go left past

St Andrews Church back towards Market Street passing St Michaels and All Angels Church. You would have noted that Bothwell's three churches are all located on the same block, which also contains a large cemetery. The earliest legible headstone in this dates back to 1834.

**14** Continue along Patrick Street past the unique Queens

Park Memorial Sundial (a rare vertical model) on the right. Across the street is the historic Castle Hotel (continually licensed since 1829) in front of which a few remaining members of the Big River Tribe are said to have staged their last corroboree on their own land. Perhaps it is time for a cuppa at the local bakery café next door before returning to your start point.

## Tasmanian history – Big River Tribe

As white settlement increasingly encroached on Aboriginal hunting grounds, conflict arose over land tenure. The indigenous population had already dwindled to less than 300 from an estimated number of 5000 to 10,000 due to the introduction of diseases such as measles and smallpox. The infamous 'Black Line' was a military plan aimed to capture remaining Aboriginals by employing large numbers of people to 'comb' settled areas and drive them out. At the same time the government agent George Augustus Robinson began a mission to 'protect' Aboriginals by rounding them up for relocation to Flinders Island. Robinson captured 16 men, nine women and one child in December, 1831. Local lore has it that they danced their last corrobboree on their land in front of the Castle Hotel in January 1832, before walking to Hobart and being transported to Flinders Island.

# 26 Historic Richmond

Time appears to have stood still in this historic village. Richmond was settled as the centre of a grain growing area, with a number of wind, water and steam driven mills. Later it also became an overnight stopping place for traffic to the east coast of Tasmania with the construction, beginning in 1823, of the Richmond Bridge across the Coal River, Australia's oldest bridge still in use. A few years later the gaol, courthouse and barracks were built. The village was bypassed in 1872 when the Sorell Causeway was completed and became the preferred route from Hobart to the east coast. The ensuing reduction in traffic though Richmond allowed the village to remain much as it was originally. On this amble through history you will find a range of buildings from simple Georgian cottages to grand two-storey residences to churches and public buildings. There are also many specialised shops to browse and places to stop for a coffee and a bite to eat.

## At a glance

**Grade:** Easy

**Time:** 1 hr

**Distance:** 2.5 km circuit

**Conditions:** Level footpaths, little shade, some street crossings

**Further information:** www.discovertasmania.com/hobart_and_surrounds

**Getting there**

**Car:** Take the Tasman Hwy out of Hobart and turn left into Cambridge then left again into Colebrook Rd to Richmond. Continue along Bridge St and turn right into Wellington St, cross over the bridge and turn left into the car park in St Johns Circle

## Walk directions

**1** Cross Wellington Street and walk towards the bridge. On your left, just before the bridge, you will pass by 'Mill House' one of the former mills mentioned in the introduction – it is now a private home.

**2** Cross the convict-built sandstone bridge and go left and uphill onto Bridge Street. Across the street you will see several quaint old cottages that now serve as bed and breakfast accommodation and the old Richmond Bakehouse dating back to 1830. On the left side you will come to Mill Cottage which is now Peppercorn Gallery, run by a cooperative of fine local artists and well worth a visit.

**3** Next on your left is the village green, where the Village Fair is held annually in autumn. The first Richmond Fair was held in 1828.

Further along you will pass the old Court House, now the Post Office and online access centre and the original Bridge Inn which operated as a hotel from 1834 to 1975. It is currently occupied by a sweet shop. A narrow lane leads from here into the Saddlers Court Complex

which also includes a very fine bakery and coffee shop and you may wish to explore this along the way.

**4** Continue along Bridge Street where you can note the timeworn flagstones in the front of the Saddlers Court Gallery which was a general store originally and later a saddlery as the name suggests.

**5** Cross Edward Street; the Village Store over the road is still just that and probably one of the oldest general stores still in use in Tasmania. Soon you will pass by the magnificently restored Richmond Arms Hotel. This site originally housed the Lennox Arms Hotel which was built in 1827. Its old stables are all that is left of it now. The prominent white double-storey building further along dates back to 1826. It began its life as a single-storey cottage which was added to in 1830 to be used as a store.

**6** Cross Henry Street and pass a row of three cottages (the first one of these was once the Star and Garter Inn, built in 1830) as the road dips downhill. At the corner of Bridge Street and Blair Street you will find Oak Lodge (c 1830), owned by the National Trust of Australia (Tasmania) and managed by the Coal River Historical Society. This building is open to visitors from 1100 to 1630 daily.

**7** Turn left into Blair Street then left into Bathurst Street. You will pass Rose Cottage (c 1840s), now a private home, which has an unusually steeply pitched roof. On the left is the former old Richmond Hotel and staging post for coaches, now a private residence.

**8** Turn right into Henry Street passing Fernville cottage. When you reach Torrens Street, cast your eye to the right to catch sight of the quaint Pop Wright's Cottage, also a private residence now. It was built in the 1840s and served as the home for the local butcher and his descendants for 126 years, from 1862 to 1988.

**9** On the corner of Torrens and Henry Streets stands The Old Schoolhouse. Built in 1834, it is the oldest State school in Australia. It is now part of the Richmond Primary School. This stone building was designed by the well-known colonial architect

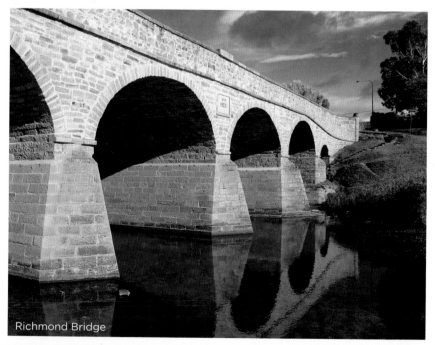

Richmond Bridge

John Lee Archer who also designed St Lukes Church (c 1834) which you will see on your right as you continue along Torrens Street. On the way you pass the Congregational burial ground and 'Emerald Cottage'.

**10** Turn left into Edward Street, pass 'The Old Rectory' (c 1831), then turn right into Bathurst Street. As you look ahead towards the Coal River, the prominent Richmond Gaol Building appears on the left. Cross the lawn towards it. It was constructed in 1825 and is well worth a visit. Open to the public from 0900 to 1700 daily (except Christmas Day). Admission is $8 for adults, $4 for children and $20 for families.

**11** Continue your walk past the Gaol and turn right just past the police station to walk through the station car park towards the Coal River. You will find a set of stone steps to take you down to the riverbank where there are picnic areas and a small wooden platform jutting into the river, a favourite spot for weddings. Walk to the bridge and pass under it, then go up the steps to the top and find your way back to the start point.

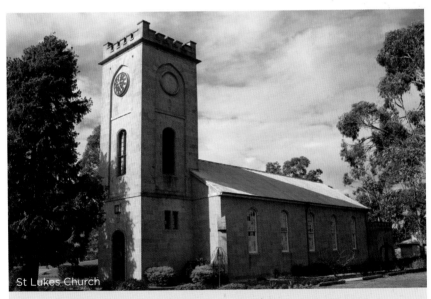

St Lukes Church

## Tasmanian history – John Lee Archer (1791-1852)

Born in Dublin, Ireland, Archer was appointed as government architect and civil engineer for Tasmania in 1826 and worked in this capacity for eleven years. During most of this time he designed all government buildings including Richmond Gaol, St Lukes Church and The Old Schoolhouse seen on this walk. His buildings were designed in the Georgian Renaissance style which is plain and solid. Among them are some buildings in the Anglesea Barracks complex, the Penitentiary Chapel, the Old Parliament House, St Georges Church in Battery Point and St Johns Church and Orphan School in New Town. These are still standing and contributing to the character of the city of Hobart and you can pay them a visit. Later in life Archer became police magistrate at Stanley, in the north-west, where he lived the rest of his life. He is buried in a small graveyard near the Nut at Stanley.

# Forest Reserves and other Protected Areas

Large tracts of Tasmanian land are administered by Forestry Tasmania as working forests. A number of small reserves have been created within these areas to preserve small samples of various types of original forest. These reserves can often be found along streams where it is a legal requirement for forestry operations to leave areas undisturbed. Four of the walks in the following chapter belong to this category, while two lead through semi-private reserves, the last of which was created by a group of volunteers. All of the walks are shady and relaxing with that true 'bush feeling' imparted by bush sounds and the distinctive aroma of the vegetation. Except for late autumn and winter you may also find many flowering plants as a bonus.

# 27 Hardings Falls

The following three pleasant, short walks are situated west of the area between the coastal towns of Bicheno and Swansea and can be accessed by travelling north or south between the two major link roads (the A4 from Conara to St Marys and the B34 from Campbell Town via Lake Leake to Swansea) giving you an alternative route to the coastal road to travel. Hardings Falls are the northernmost; Meetus Falls are approximately halfway to Lost Falls which are the southernmost. Hardings Falls, in the Swan River, consists of a number of small waterfalls in the Swan River tumbling over dolerite shelves.

## At a glance

**Grade:** Medium

**Time:** 1 hr

**Distance:** 1.2 km circuit

**Ascent/Descent:** 60 m/60 m

**Conditions:** Steep and rocky section; some log obstacles

### Getting there

**Car:** From the Tasman Hwy (A3) turn off at Cranbrook into the Old Coach Road (C301) which leads to Royal George and Avoca. Drive about 19 km to a 4-way junction, turn right into MG forestry road (also known as McKays Rd), after about 7 kilometres turn right again and drive 2 kilometres to the signposted car park

Hardings Falls

## Walk directions

**1** The track heads off level through tall banksias, bull oaks and white gums. You will hear wattlebirds above. In the understorey are saggs and sedges. Directly you will reach a Y-junction. Turn left to Riverside Loop. Take care to relocate the track after walking around fallen trees. You will note that the forest here is dry sclerophyll, and jack jumpers can be seen.

**2** The track dips down sidling along the hill. As you pass the base of a small, broken-off dolerite column, the wide, rocky riverbed comes into view. The vegetation becomes denser with wet forest species such as

Tasmanian blanket leaf and blackwood making an appearance.

**3** The track becomes rocky and further down you will find a sign giving you the option of *Top of Falls* or *Base of Falls*. Continue downhill in the *Top of Falls* direction and soon you will emerge at a rockpool and the top of the falls.

**4** This is a lovely spot to rest a while and inspect the bedrock shelves and surrounding pool.

**5** Return to the last track junction and sharply turn left on the

switchback that directs you to the *Base of Falls*. At time of writing two massive banksias had fallen across the track and needed to be circumnavigated. This is not too difficult if you bear in mind that the track continues more or less along the contour of the hill. There are two more fallen logs to negotiate before the now clear track goes up and soon you will gain lovely views upstream to the top of the falls and across the river to some fine dolerite columns, making the trouble to get here worthwhile.

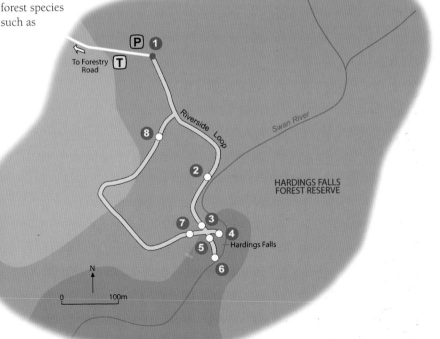

**6** Turn left at a signed turn-off to go to the base of the falls. Initially the climb is very steep and rocky, but the narrow track is well built and easier than it first appears. However you need to be able to do a bit of rock-hopping near the base where there is a large gum with a burl hugging the boulders in the river. Some interesting plants along the way are sunshine wattle and the endemic Tasmanian speedwell with its beautiful four-petalled pale lilac or white flowers.

**7** Return to the top of the escarpment and at the Y-junction you passed earlier, go straight ahead uphill in a gentler climb which leads through blackwood and bracken fern with *Eucalyptus delegatensis* above.

**8** Soon you will reach the end of the Riverside Loop. Turn left here to go back to the start point.

## Tasmanian flora – Sunshine wattle (*Acacia terminalis*)

This attractive, tricky little wattle is very adaptable and therefore widespread in Australia. It can be found from northern New South Wales to Tasmania. However, you may not always recognise it, as it can appear as a small shrub but also as a tree up to five or six metres tall. The colour of its flowers ranges from cream to bright yellow and it tends to flower at odd times from autumn to mid-spring. Sunshine wattle prefers open woodland and will grow in a range of soil types. The best way to identify it is by its dark green, fern-like (bipinnate) leaves.

Botanists have had trouble with the classification of the sunshine wattle and have renamed it several times. It started off as *Mimosa terminalis* a long time ago. It was then re-classified as a wattle or *Acacia* and became *Acacia discolor* (which means 'two-coloured' and may refer to its seed pods). Botanists then renamed it *Acacia botrycephala* which means 'clustered head'. Perhaps botanists then decided that this was too hard to pronounce (just the author's opinion!) and re-renamed it *Acacia terminalis*, which similarly refers to the fact that it carries its flowers on the end of branchlets (terminate – to end).

Top of Hardings Falls

# 28 Meetus Falls

From the well-appointed picnic area and car park the track starts off in dry sclerophyll forest. As you descend to the Cygnet River you will encounter wet forest species and ferns. The falls are spectacular at any time but obviously more so after rain.

## At a glance

**Grade:** Easy

**Time:** 45 mins

**Distance:** 1 km return

**Ascent/Descent:** 80 m/80 m

**Conditions:** Easy to follow well-built foot track; steep, damp sections; mostly shady

### Getting there

**Car:** From the Tasman Hwy (A3) turn left into the Lake Leake Road (B34) 10 kilometres north of Swansea. After about 20 kilometres turn right into the M forest road. After about 10 kilometres turn right into the access road to Meetus Falls and drive to its end. Alternately if travelling south from Hardings Falls return to 4-way junction and continue straight ahead (south-west) on the M road (also known as McKays Rd) until you reach the Meetus Falls access road on your left

## Walk directions

**1** Your walk begins on the left side of the picnic shelter and is signed *Falls Lookout and Cygnet River*. The track is rocky and leads through similar terrain as described for Lost Falls, with guitar plants, bracken fern and blue Tasmanian flax lily growing amongst the rocks in the understorey with a *Eucalyptus delegatensis* canopy.

**2** The track leads up a small rise before dipping down into the river valley. Soon you'll see various fern species appearing on the forest floor. The track becomes steeper before a signed Y-junction.

**3** Go right to the Falls Lookout passing through wet forest vegetation. A set of wooden steps will take you to the lookout. After rain these falls are particularly impressive as they tumble some 40 metres down the dolerite cliff face.

**4** Return to the junction and make your way downhill to the Cygnet River. The forest gradually turns denser with a much taller understorey. The track becomes steep and less rocky with many ferns and mosses lining its edges. Although there are no track markers, the path is clearly visible. You

N

0      100m

**MEETUS FALLS FOREST RESERVE**

*Cygnet River*

*Meetus Falls*

may hear kookaburras overhead as you pass a particularly massive gum tree on the left side of the track.

**5** Soon you will reach a beautiful stand of manferns interplanted with the wet forest species, sassafras, silver wattle and dogwoods.

**6** After a while the track swings to the right as it zigzags its way down towards the river leading through fishtail fern. The sound of rushing water increases as you near the base of the falls. Eventually you reach a sign announcing *Cygnet River – Base of Falls* and warning you of slippery rocks.

**7** Enjoy the falls and return to the start point by the same route.

## Tasmanian flora – Manfern or Soft Tree Fern (*Dicksonia antarctica*)

These giants of the fern world are endemic to Australia and can be found in cool areas with high rainfall in south-eastern parts of the continent. They can reach heights of up to 15 metres with fronds up to three metres long. But they don't do this overnight: they grow very slowly, only one to ten centimetres per year, depending on conditions. Their 'trunks' are actually rhizomes or a type of root. The manfern's ancestry goes back to times when the first ferns appeared on our planet about 300 million years ago. Fossil evidence shows that they were part of the so-called Antarctic flora on the Gondwanan supercontinent which at that time consisted of Australia, New Zealand, Antarctica, South America, Africa, Madagascar and India. In those days long ago, Antarctica was covered in vegetation which is a bit hard to imagine now that the supercontinent has broken up and Antarctica has been left in the cold.

# 29 Lost Falls and Scenic Lookout

Although the following walk is only short, this little known forest reserve is well worth a visit, especially if you can combine it with walks to Meetus and Hardings Falls, which are situated nearby to the north. The lookout is easily reached and has lovely views into the densely forested, steep-sided Lost Falls Creek below. A gentle climb to the scenic lookout to the east of the car park to a dolerite platform rewards you with splendid views to the coast and Freycinet Peninsula.

Lost Falls

## At a glance

**Grade:** Easy

**Time:** 45 mins

**Distance:** 1.3 km return

**Ascent/Descent:** 80 m/80 m

**Conditions:** Well-made track.

**Getting there**
**Car:** From the Tasman Hwy (A3) turn left into Lake Leake Road (B34) 10 kilometres north of Swansea. After about 20 kilometres turn left into the MS forest road (also known as McKays Rd). After about 5 kilometres turn left into the signed road (Crossing Rd). Alternatively, if travelling south from Meetus Falls cross Lake Leake Road (B34) and continue for 5 kilometres, then turn left into Crossing Road. Continue along this road until you reach the Lost Falls carpark

## Walk directions

**1** Locate the narrow, gravelled, rocky, signed foot track which leads off the right side of the turning circle. The track dips down through lichen-covered rocks with native cherry, guitar plant and berry bush growing nearby. You soon hear the sound of rushing water as you reach a Y-junction.

**2** Go left to the lookout. The understorey now contains narrow-leafed wattle and banksia. Only a few steps along you will find the fenced lookout perched atop a steep cliff. From it you can look down into the steep gully which has been gouged into the dolerite by Lost Falls Creek, which runs towards the coast in a south-easterly direction.

**3** Carefully make your way along the unfenced cliff top to the next lookout which is only a few metres away. As you look down into the abyss, you will see the falls on the bare rock beneath with dolerite columns towering above them.

**4** Retrace your steps to the Y-junction and continue downhill to the River Pools. Directly you will catch a glimpse of some fine examples of columnar dolerite across the river valley. The track dips down at this stage and the vegetation changes to reflect the moister conditions in this area. You may be able to spot dogwoods, saggs and the beautiful tubular bells of wild fuchsia among the moss and lichen-covered rocks.

LOST FALLS FOREST RESERVE

Lost Falls Creek

Coastal Scenic View Track

0    100m

**5** The track becomes very rocky here as you pass some large boulders. Shortly it emerges at the first rockpool on the left and a little further along you can find a number of smaller rockpools as the track ends.

**6** Return to the turning circle for the second half of your walk.

Take the signed track *Coastal Scenic View* which winds up a small rocky knoll through open dry bushland to a small, solid dolerite plateau.

**7** Cross the little plateau to another larger one where some amateur rock cairn building has obviously been practised by some earlier visitors! From

## Tasmanian flora – Leptospermum grandiflorum

This plant does not appear to have a common name but most of us can easily translate its name into 'grand-flowered' tea-tree. It is endemic to Tasmania and is a large shrub which is not commonly seen, preferring relatively undisturbed sites with a high rainfall. It is found on the east coast of Tasmania and is easily identified, as the beautiful white flowers and the seed capsules are much larger than those of other tea-tree species.

here, on a clear day, you can see as far as Freycinet Peninsula to the north-east and to the south-east into the steep Lost Falls River valley you have just visited. Some plants to look for are hakea, necklace she-oak and the rare tea-tree *Leptospermum grandiflorum*.

After having enjoyed the view and perhaps tried your hand at cairn building, return to the start point.

# 30 Tasmanian Bushland Garden

This garden is one of a series of Regional Botanic Gardens in Australia where the local flora of a specific area is displayed. Within this 20-hectare reserve you will find a large collection of south-eastern Tasmania's indigenous plants from various soil types showcased and interpreted in an interesting garden setting. Picnic facilities and interpretive signage invite you to linger before or after you have enjoyed a walk through the natural bushland that surrounds the display garden. From a lookout at the highest point on your walk you will be able to see as far as the Three Thumbs on the East Coast.

## At a glance

**Grade:** Easy

**Time:** Allow 1 hr

**Distance:** 1.4 km circuit

**Ascent/Descent:** 60 m/60 m

**Conditions:** Narrow bush track with rocky, steep section, mostly shady. Opening hours, Oct–Mar 0800-1800, Apr–Sep 0900-1600; donations welcome

**Further information:** Pulchella Nursery, T (03) 6257 5189

### Getting there

**Car:** From Hobart take the Tasman Highway (A3 across the Tasman Bridge to Sorell). Turn left to continue towards Orford. 2.8 kilometres after passing Break me Neck Hill turn right into signed Tasmanian Bushland Garden to park in a designated parking area. Coming from the East Coast, turn left 4.2 kilometres west of Buckland

## Walk directions

**1** From the car park cross the garden area towards a couple of waterholes. Walk past these, leaving them to your right, and locate a gate in the vermin-proof fence that surrounds the garden area.

**2** Enter the bushland through the gate, making sure to close it behind you. The track passes under the canopy of a stand of magnificent white gums and leads downhill following a small watercourse.

**3** Keep right at a Y-junction on a short side track which rejoins

the main track a little further down the hill. The understorey in this area is dominated by poa grasses, saggs, black wattle and pink berry.

Black peppermint appears among the white gums. The track becomes rockier.

**4** Just before a small footbridge, keep right on a short access to view Nelson Creek at a lovely shady resting spot.

**5** Return to the main track by crossing the footbridge and continue along it as it curves to the left to skirt the low hill that forms the centre of this small bushland block. The track becomes very rough and rocky as you ascend the hill across a small dolerite scree. Up higher you will be able to spot Nelson Creek below on your right and also beyond its riparian vegetation the neighbouring bush run which is still grazed by sheep. The vegetation in this area receives much shade and you will see blanket bush and Tasmanian flax lily. The latter loves rocky hillsides and forms clumps with its strap-like, slightly serrated leaves. It bears blue flowers with prominent yellow stamens in spring and blue berries in autumn.

TASMANIAN BUSHLAND GARDEN

Tasman Hwy

P 1

T

10

9

Hill Top

Loop

Track

8

Wallaby Track

7

N

0 100m

2

3

White Gum Loop

Wombat Track

6

5

4

Nelson Creek

Pulchella Nursery

**6** After a short while the track levels and follows the boundary fence on the right. The bush becomes sparser and drier with tussocks and wattles dominating. On your right you will soon note a particularly healthy stand of yellow bottlebrush.

**7** The track begins to curve left and becomes slightly indistinct as it rises steeply towards the hilltop past a beautiful native cherry. Follow the white marker posts as you go up, the last few metres are quite steep.

**8** After this short climb you will emerge on the small plateau where the native silver tussock grasses and associated herbaceous plants are regenerating from heavy grazing by sheep last century.

## Tasmanian environment – Dolerite

Dolerite, also known as 'bluestone', or 'blue metal' in its crushed form, is rare worldwide but abundant in Tasmania. Approximately half the area of Tasmania is underlain by Jurassic dolerite. Subsequent weathering has exposed much of the dolerite's columnar structure giving many of Tasmania's mountains, including Mount Wellington, their characteristic 'organ pipe' appearance.

The area above the picnic shelter at the Bushland Garden was once a dolerite quarry. Blue metal has been quarried in Tasmania since early colonisation to pave roads. Today it is mainly used as crushed aggregate in concrete production, as a road sub-base and combined with tar for road surfacing.

**9** A seat at a lookout point allows you to rest and contemplate the fine views to the east coast. The Tasman Highway heading towards Buckland is clearly visible in the foreground.

**10** To complete your walk continue along the loop track to descend a dry rocky slope with small boulders, a favourite hiding place for echidnas. The track heads for a gate in the vermin-proof fence allowing you

to re-enter the garden area and return to the car park and your start point. After passing through the gate you will note some tall bushes with dark green leaves – the native hop bush.

## Tasmanian fauna – White's skink (*Egernia whitii*)

As you wander around the Bushland Garden you may have noticed many little lizards sunning themselves on the rocks and scurrying away at great speed on your approach. Tasmania has eleven species of lizards, more correctly named skinks. One of the prettiest is White's skink which can be found in northern and

eastern Tasmania at altitudes below 400 metres. The skinks dig burrows with two entrances, under or between rock slabs or logs and prefer sunny areas. Several of them may share the accommodation. Their diet consists of small invertebrates such as ants, leaf-hoppers, spiders, and millipedes with the occasional addition of a green salad. They have a relatively long life span, up to eight years or so, and give birth to one to five live young in February.

# 31 Woodvine Reserve

Combine a rare glimpse into Tasmania's early farming history with a pleasant walk through species-rich open forest, giving you an idea of what the land must have been like before it was cleared for farming. Through the trees at the end of the track you can enjoy views out towards Marion Bay. Before you set off on your walk you may be tempted to inspect the historic farm buildings and other remaining artefacts around the house paddock which will give you an insight into the way of life of early settlers, their frugal, self-sufficient lifestyle and resourceful 'make do' attitude. This is an easy walk, which follows an old farm track. Large areas of bush on Woodvine were burnt during the terrible bushfires in January 2013 which originated at Forcett and largely destroyed Dunally and the Forestier Peninsula.

## At a glance

**Grade:** Easy

**Time:** 1 hr 30 mins

**Distance:** 5 km

**Ascent/Descent:** 20m

**Conditions:** Old farm track, partly shaded

**Further information:** Parks and Wildlife Service, Seven Mile Beach, T (03) 6214 8100

### Getting there

**Car:** Take the Tasman Highway (A3). At Forcett turn left into Delmore Rd (signed Wattle Hill). After 1 kilometre turn right into White Hill Rd and follow it to the end (about 7 kilometres) and park (avoid the space under large pine trees as they may drop cones and dent your car!)

## Walk directions

**1** Enter the house paddock through a special gap in the main gate. Immediately turn right to follow the old, sandy, overgrown farm track along Woodvine's southern boundary fence. You will notice some beautiful blackwoods growing along the fence line. On your left, across the old paddocks, are wide views to the beautiful bushland and the hills beyond. Soon you will pass under tall gums with an understorey of banksia and the odd native cherry tree and in a lower spot tea-tree and saggs.

**2** Shortly you will reach a boot cleaning station. Two old hearth brushes tied to fence posts are provided to brush the soles of your boots and remove any weed seeds (particularly Spanish heath) adhering to them. Your help here will significantly reduce the workload for volunteers who are hoping

to control this horribly invasive weed. Continue along the track past a small marshy area containing coral fern, sword sedge and buttongrass.

**3** After a little over half an hour of walking the track will begin to rise gradually to an altitude of about 231 metres.

**4** The substantial hill you can soon see from the top of a

rise up ahead is known as Mother Browns Bonnet. A gentle slope down and a gradual curve towards the south-east leads to another marshy spot with tall gums such as black peppermint and brown top stringybark enjoying the extra moisture. As you leave the small marsh you will note a change in the soil, which now supports silver peppermints creating lovely dappled shade with their sparse silvery foliage.

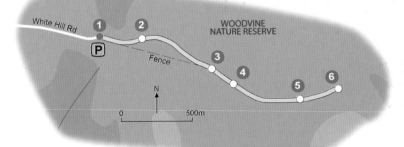

**5** You will pass an old fence line with a strainer post still standing on your left, then cross a watercourse before another rise.

**6** Finally you will reach the highest point in the fading farm track and will be able to enjoy the view through the open forest across the neighbouring farmland below. Many wildflowers can be found growing among the grass, such as orchids, bluebells and native violets. Birds and butterflies abound as well. After having enjoyed the views, carefully retrace your steps to the start.

## Tasmanian history – Early settlers

Woodvine has been held by members of the same family since it was selected by Daniel and Elizabeth Long in 1861. Elizabeth was a midwife and bore 14 children. The second last, Oswald Charles Bertram, died as an infant; a plaque marks his grave site.

Three cottages were built on Woodvine over time. The first was a shingle-roofed slab construction which was later converted to a shearing shed. The second home, built circa 1890, has a corrugated iron hip roof and is clad with weatherboards. There is a lean-to at its rear and a large sandstone chimney on one side. The third home dates to 1902 and is partly clad with cement sheeting. It was occupied by Bernie Shaw, a great-grandson of Daniel and Elizabeth Long, until 2003. Bernie donated Woodvine to the Crown in 1998. It was proclaimed a Nature Reserve three years later.

Most of the cultural heritage has been moved to the Tasmanian Museum and Art Gallery for safekeeping.

### Tasmanian flora – Spanish or Portuguese heath (*Erica lusitanica*)

Native to south-eastern Europe this plant has migrated to most other parts of the world and become a weed. It belongs to the heather family of plants, is woody and evergreen and can grow up to two metres tall. It has light green, needle-like leaves. Its dense clusters of pretty, tiny bell-shaped white or pink flowers are capable of producing up to nine million dust-like seeds per plant and of course this is transported very readily. Seed can remain viable for many years, so it is no wonder you are asked to **please** brush your boots when walking from an infested area into pristine bushland.

# 32 Chauncy Vale to Flat Rock Lookout

The main attraction of this area is the diverse flora which is internationally recognised as a biodiversity hotspot with a high concentration of endemic and threatened species. You will have the chance to walk through remnant stands of silver peppermint and grassy blue gum forests and see rock plate grasslands clothed in threatened annual plant species and orchids. This walk is a delight even for the non-botanist and you are rewarded with panoramic and little known views of Tasmania's Southern Midlands from the lookout on top of Flat Rock.

View from Flat Rock

## At a glance

**Grade:** Medium

**Time:** 5 hrs

**Distance:** 11 km return

**Ascent/Descent:** 340 m/340 m

**Conditions:** Narrow bush track along creek with some crossings (not negotiable during flood times) then mostly old logging tracks beneath open bushland

**Further information:** Chauncy Vale Wildlife Sanctuary Caretaker, T (03) 6268 6365; Tasmanian Land Conservancy, tasland.org.au

**Getting there**

**Car:** Take the Midland Highway to Bagdad, turn right into signposted Chauncy Vale Road. Drive to the road's end and through gate, shutting it behind you. Donations are accepted at the gate. Park car in designated parking area by information shelter

## Walk directions

**1** Continue along the driveway which leads past a large grassed area with a picnic shelter and gas barbecue. A little further along you will find a hut with a walker registration book inside, a bush toilet and a quaint garden gate through which your walking track begins.

**2** A few metres from the gate a panel (oddly facing away from you) depicts a map of the reserve. Keep left at the nearby Y-junction with a directional sign for various walking tracks on the reserve (some of which you may like to undertake later). Pass a grassy area to a crossing of Browns Caves Creek then follow this watercourse. Typical river bank vegetation shades the track here, including blackwood, dogwood and native olive.

**3** When you reach the junction with the Caves Track (of Nan Chauncy's *They found a Cave* fame), go left. You will note Eve's Bath (a bath-shaped rock formation in the creek) on your right.

**4** Recross the creek a little later and pass a nasty infestation of perennial Californian thistles to reach a large boulder and beautiful native cherry tree on your right where the return loop from Browns Caves rejoins the track.

**5** Keep left to cross the creek for the last time before you begin to climb along a valley formed by a tributary to Browns Caves Creek. You will hear many birds in the tall trees above and perhaps chance upon some Bennett's wallabies. Soon you will reach a small dolerite scree. Ignore a faint vehicle track to the right.

**6** At the junction with Guvys Lagoon Track keep left to follow the northerly route to Flat Rock which is marked with blue tape here. It leads to the top of a ridge that extends north from Devils Elbow, the prominent 500-metre hill you are sidling along.

## Tasmanian environment – Flat Rock Reserve

This 455-hectare reserve, consisting of part of a range of flat dolerite-covered hills, abuts the northern boundary of Chauncy Vale and links with the Alpha Pinnacle Conservation Area to its north-east. The area was logged by Gunns Limited until the 1980s. Later it was jointly purchased by the Southern Midlands Council and the community group Friends of Chauncy Vale with help from the Tasmanian Land Conservancy (TLC).

**7** Silver peppermints, named for their silvery leaves, buds and trunks, grow in the well-drained Permian mudstone soils which are their preferred habitat. As you have gained about 140 metres in height from the start point, views towards Bagdad and the Midland Highway will gradually appear to the south-west with Mangalore Tier on the skyline. When you reach the top of the ridge, keep left to skirt around the top of the tributary.

**8** Go right at a T-junction to continue in a northerly direction, following the sparse blue tape markers until you see a yellow sign on the boundary of Chauncy Vale with Flat Rock Reserve with the heading *Conservation Area*. Turn right at the next junction to pass through a beautiful moist gully where banksias, silver wattles, prickly wattle, tea-tree, dogwood, cheeseberry, ferns and Tasmanian flax lily grow, to name just a few of the very rich flora in this area. Watch out for interesting birds here as well; you may see or hear fan-tailed cuckoos, grey shrike thrush, yellow-throated honeyeaters, golden whistlers, black-headed honeyeaters, grey fantails and black currawongs (or mountain jays).

**9** Keep left at the next two junctions. The bush has regrown well here since logging days. Large tree stumps remain to tell a story. Shortly the track joins a more major road by a wooden yellow post marker.

**10** Turn left and downhill to lead you to the Western Lookout. You pass through a grassy blue gum area which gives way to the flat dolerite cap. A small rock cairn marks a left turn

## Tasmanian environment – TLC

This organisation was founded in 2001 with the aim of protecting endangered species habitats and rare ecosystems in three different ways; as permanent reserves to be managed by the TLC, through a revolving fund where private land is purchased by the TLC, covenanted and re-sold to sympathetic buyers and thirdly through work with existing landowners to help them access funds from government and corporate sponsors for the protection of environmental values on their own land. The TLC also receives private donations. It is run by a few paid staff and an army of volunteers.

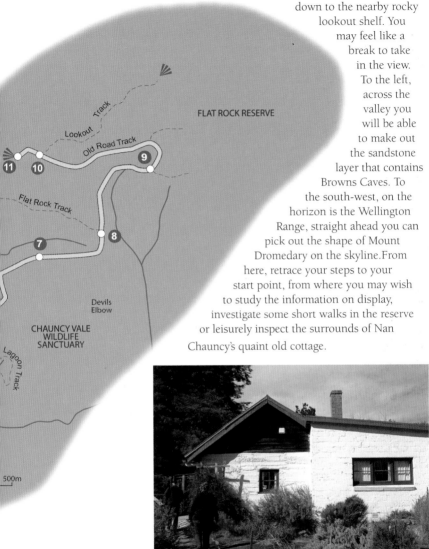

FLAT ROCK RESERVE

Lookout Track

Old Road Track

Flat Rock Track

9

11 10

7 8

Devils Elbow

CHAUNCY VALE WILDLIFE SANCTUARY

Lagoon Track

500m

down to the nearby rocky lookout shelf. You may feel like a break to take in the view. To the left, across the valley you will be able to make out the sandstone layer that contains Browns Caves. To the south-west, on the horizon is the Wellington Range, straight ahead you can pick out the shape of Mount Dromedary on the skyline. From here, retrace your steps to your start point, from where you may wish to study the information on display, investigate some short walks in the reserve or leisurely inspect the surrounds of Nan Chauncy's quaint old cottage.

Chauncy's home

## Tasmanian history – *They Found a Cave*

Browns Cave at Chauncy Vale is said to have inspired the children's author Nan Chauncy, whose home can be seen near the entrance gate to the reserve, to pen her first novel in 1948. *They Found a Cave,* which was about a bushranger hiding out in a cave, was highly acclaimed. Nan's realistic writing style and portrayal of children was seen as innovative and fresh. She subsequently wrote eleven popular novels, some of which introduced Tasmanian Aboriginal themes. Nan died in 1970 and the sanctuary was bequeathed to the local council by her husband Anton in 1988.

# The Far South

Although, strictly speaking, not all of the following walks are south of Hobart, they are reached by leaving Hobart on the Southern Outlet which connects the city to Kingston, the Huon Valley and Tasmania's southernmost areas. The drive to start these walks is often very pleasant in itself as it leads through rich orchard, cropping and farming land that enjoys a higher rainfall than the dryer Midlands and East Coast. Tasmania's Southern Mountains, with tall forests in their foothills, form a magnificent backdrop to the west, while there are delightful water views to the east. The range of walks in this chapter includes small forays to the edge of these mountains and, after you have driven as far south as you can drive in Australia, a relaxing coastal walk that takes in some of Tasmania's early whaling history. And for your return to Hobart, a lovely walk from Montrose to the very popular MONA museum has been included.

# 33 Mount Misery

Not a misery at all, this pleasant walk starts at the Huon Bush Retreats accommodation and camping complex in a forest setting. It leads through wet forest and rainforest with large stands of manfern to a sandstone plateau, clothed in heath, that allows views to the south-west wilderness. Crossing the plateau and a saddle you will reach a rocky outcrop with a miserable face! Retrace your steps for much of the way, enjoying the different view you see facing downhill and finish with a visit to a live tree gutted by fire, and a small waterfall.

## At a glance

**Grade:** Medium

**Time:** 3 hrs 30 mins

**Distance:** 6.2 km return

**Ascent/Descent:** 280 m/280 m, waterfall 50 m/50 m

**Conditions:** Walking track is well built (by Greencorps and Woofer volunteers) with moist and shady sections, stone steps and some duckboarding. Upper section can be very exposed in poor weather

**Further information:**
www.huonbushretreats.com

**Getting there**

**Car:** From Hobart take the Southern Outlet (A6) and follow signage towards Huonville. 3 kilometres south of Grove turn right towards Judbury. Pass through Ranelagh. Turn right into Browns Road after 2.5 kilometres, follow this steep gravel road for 3 kilometres to front gate of reserve and another 1 kilometre to reception. Pass reception and park in a designated day visitor park near picnic shelter

## Walk directions

**1** Locate the start of the walk to the left of the picnic shelter, with walker registration. The track leads uphill through dense mixed forest with an understorey of bracken fern and soon curves to the left. You will see evidence of the massive logs that have been taken from here in the past and of the devastating 1967 bushfires where much of Tasmania, including this area, was burnt. The oldest trees here have therefore grown from seedlings dispersed at that time. You will note that subsequent generations of trees have produced offspring since. The bracken fern in the understorey still belongs to the first succession of plants after the fire.

**2** Soon a sprinkling of tree ferns appears along the track, gradually thickening as you progress, particularly in the gully to your left. Wet spots contain cutting grass and blanket bush. Sections of the track here are 'paved' with bush stones and soon you will note some truly gigantic eucalypts, the mighty swamp gum (*Eucalyptus regnans*), thought to be about 350 years old, as well as some numbered markers appearing beside the track. Their presence is explained at the next track junction: a sighting device, with instructions on how to use it, shows you how to estimate the height of these forest giants.

**3** Turn left and go downhill to continue your walk. The track loops right, past a large eucalypt sporting impressive burls, to a wooden platform.

**4** A few metres along you will reach the turn-off to Mount Misery, with the loop continuing back down to the Bush Retreat. Turn right and go uphill, passing over and under large mossy logs that have fallen long ago. Where a small watercourse crosses the track, some wooden steps and a platform have been built and there is a lovely seat for a rest to enjoy the ferny forest.

**5** The track rises more steeply from here, leading up well-built stone steps. As you climb higher you will begin to glimpse views through the trees, down to the valley below. The track curves right and soon begins to zigzag

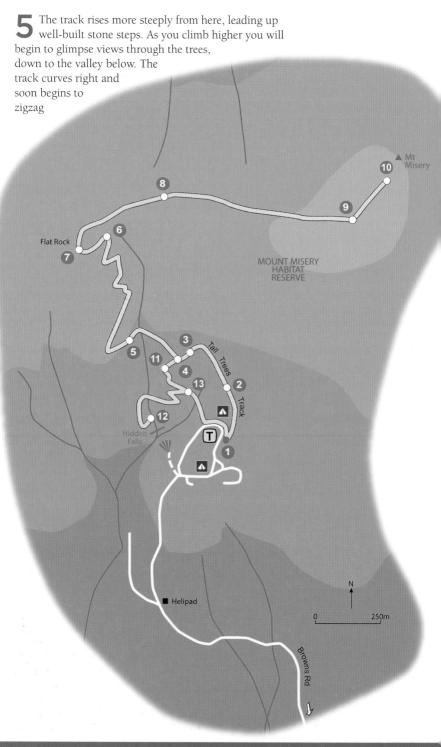

Flat Rock

MOUNT MISERY
HABITAT
RESERVE

Tall Trees Track

Hidden Falls

▲ Mt Misery

N

0        250m

Browns Rd

■ Helipad

uphill through an area of rainforest species. You may be able to spot the dainty leaves of myrtle and the shiny, dark green, toothed leaves of sassafras, both very prominent rainforest trees. In autumn a number of interesting fungi grow on the forest floor. A low, moss-covered cliff will appear on your left with the track leading to its top. Not far away is Regnans Lookout which is gated and has some interpretive signage.

**6** Passing a more exposed sandstone shelf with interpretive signage you ascend to its top and emerge onto a clear, sub-alpine plateau covered in heath. Plants are stunted here due to exposure to cold and wind, and to the shallow soils that barely cover the sandstone bedrock and are waterlogged due to poor drainage. About 300 hectares of this area was burnt during a bushfire in 2006 and you will note how this has given smaller plants such as the beautiful trigger plant a chance to colonise in large numbers. No doubt this will change in future years as the regrowth of tea-tree and banksias becomes taller and shades the ground.

**7** The track leads to Flat Rock, atop Fletchers Hill, then loops to the right in a north-easterly direction to cross a low saddle with open eucalypt forest that also bears the scars of the 2006 fire.

**8** For the final leg to the top you pass through a heathland of taller tea-trees, banksias and melaleucas. The mounds beside the track are made by jack jumpers, so take care not to step on them.

**9** Cross a wetter spot with cutting grass, coral fern and bauera.

**10** Pass a closed-off track on the right (this is on private land and leads to the trig on top of the true summit) before climbing the last rockier section to several large boulders that overlook the valley below. Don't forget to look for the 'miserable face' attached to one of the boulders!

**11** Retrace your steps to the T-junction back in the ferny gully and turn

Coral fungi

Lightning Tree

right here. Shortly you will cross an enormous log via a purpose-built 'stile' then go downhill along another huge log. The track has stone steps at intervals to prevent erosion.

**12** Turn right at the next junction for a small side trip through the Lightning Tree and down to the small viewing platform and seat that overlook the gully and the Hidden Falls.

**13** Return to the junction and turn right to emerge at the Bush Retreat road a few minutes later. Go left, past a large amenities block, to find your start point.

Mount Misery summit

## Tasmanian environment – Burls

These sometimes very large, knotty and rather grotesque growths on the outside of tree trunks of various forest trees, such as myrtle and eucalypt, could be likened to scar tissue. They only occur on susceptible species such as blue gum *(Eucalyptus globulus)* and shining gum *(Eucalyptus nitens)*. It is thought that they are formed in response to an injury; hence they are also known as wound wood and have an anti-microbial role. Burls seal off the wound site, restrict the spread of an infection and re-establish the flow of sap.

Prized by artisans, burls are often crafted into beautiful objects such as dishes, bowls and clock faces. You can find these at markets and craft fairs.

# 34 Billy Browns Falls

Three retired local residents have worked to create the last section of this track which initially leads along a forestry road then up and over the top of a spur into a valley cut by a tributary to Judds Creek, where you can see the falls tumble over a thirty to forty metre escarpment into the valley below.

Judds Creek

## At a glance

**Grade:** Hard

**Time:** 5 hrs

**Distance:** 8 km return

**Ascent/Descent:** 450 m/450 m

**Conditions:** Steep forestry road, steep, rough, shaded bush track, unmarked but fairly easy to follow; a lot of downhill for the return!

### Getting there

**Car:** From Hobart take the Southern Outlet (A6). Turn right into Ranelagh/Judbury Rd (C619). At Ranelagh take a right turn into North Huon Rd to Judbury. At Judbury turn right into Judds Creek Rd. After about 8 kilometres, park car just before Judds Creek crossing. If you are lucky enough to own a 4WD vehicle you can continue along the road to point 8, cutting walking time approximately in half, but that would be cheating yourself of an invigorating forest walk!

## Walk directions

**1** Begin your walk by crossing Judds Creek and walking along the forestry road which initially follows the creek, then curves left and crosses it.

**2** As you ascend steeply along the road you leave Judds Creek way below in a narrow gully. This area receives a high rainfall and is also on a south-facing slope where plants are shaded for much of the time. You will see plant species that thrive under these conditions, such as daisy bush, blanket leaf and dogwood. The gully on your left is filled with manferns.

**3** Soon the road veers right and further away from the creek, continuing to climb steadily. A steep-sided gully now appears on your right. Some very gnarled old blanket leaf plants line the roadside.

**4** After about 15 to 20 minutes a short level section allows you to briefly catch your breath. A couple of huge tree stumps in the regrowth forest are reminders of the forest giants that once grew here.

**5** You will pass a turn-off on the left and cross a fern-lined creek rushing down to meet Judds Creek.

**6** Fishbone fern also grows on the roadside as you continue uphill. Silver wattle, native laurel and the occasional myrtle can be found here beneath the tall eucalypts.

**7** Keep right at a road junction and turning circle and pass a patch of cutting grass.

**8** Shortly you will reach another junction. Keeping right again you will note a sign about 100 metres along on your right which marks the entrance to an old logging track. It rises steeply through wet regrowth forest with cutting grass and dogwood in the understorey. You will pass another large stump of a former forest giant.

**9** As you climb further, you will find a sprinkling of manferns among the eucalypts

*Judds Creek*

To
Judds
Creek Rd

N

0          250m

Billy
Browns
Falls

and blanket leaf. This area is home to many birds including the olive whistler and the Tasmanian endemic scrub tit which you may be lucky enough to see and hear during your walk.

**10** Some very large gums tower above and pink berry, cheeseberry and native laurel can be found in the understorey.

**11** You will reach the top of the ridge in about 20 minutes. There is a beautiful stand of mature dogwood and blanket leaf in this area which form an unusual canopy.

**12** After topping the ridge the track dips down steeply in a south-easterly direction towards the falls. The rocks that line the track have an interesting covering of mosses and lichen. You may note the odd sassafras tree, which yields timber prized by artisans and

## Tasmanian birdlife – Olive whistler (*Pachycephala olivacea*)

As their name suggests, these birds have a repertoire of beautiful and distinctive whistling songs that can be heard from afar. They can be found in most of south-eastern Australia, Tasmania included, in wet forests, rainforests, woodlands and alpine heaths. Olive whistlers feed on arboreal and ground-dwelling insects and other invertebrates, and supplement this diet with berries. Both parents build shallow cup-shaped nests from twigs, bark, grasses, roots and leaves about two metres from the ground. Two to three creamy coloured eggs with brown blotches are laid and both parents share the job of incubating and feeding their chicks once they have hatched.

Billy Browns Falls

furniture makers for its beautiful dark figuring which is thought to be caused by a fungus.

**13** Directly you will hear the sound of water rushing down the falls and you will emerge on a rock platform below the falls minutes later. This is a lovely, cool shady spot to rest before your return to the start.

### Tasmanian fauna – Brush-tailed possum (*Trichosurus vulpecular*)

Most people are familiar with this nocturnal, cat-sized marsupial which has adapted well to life among humans. Possums have learnt to utilise roof spaces and garden sheds as their housing and to dine on backyard garden produce with a preference for rose bushes and fruit trees. They will raid campsites and rubbish bins as well. In Tasmania possums also quite often graze on grass. In the bush, brush-tailed possums feed on leaves, buds, flowers and fruits. They have strong teeth and often use their front paws to hold their food while eating. Possum fur is very thick and comes in a range of colours from blackish to brownish to grey, and even to rare blonde individuals. Their tails are black and naked on the underside. They lead a largely solitary life, but can get very vocal at night, making screeching and guttural cackling noises at each other to defend their territory or favourite rose bush.

# 35 Lake Skinner

Much of this walk leads through open forest where a wonderful array of wildflowers can be found. During spring and summer you may delight in the masses of bold, bright red Tasmanian waratah in the understorey, whereas in autumn the exquisitely dainty red flowers of Tasmanian climbing heath will catch your eye. A steady climb takes you to the beautiful, deep lake which was formed by glaciations. The weather can change rapidly and often a very cold blast comes down from the Snowy Range which towers above Lake Skinner.

Lake Skinner

## At a glance

**Grade:** Hard

**Time:** 5 hrs 30 mins

**Distance:** 8.8 km return

**Ascent/Descent:** 460 m /460 m

**Conditions:** Easy to follow, fairly distinct track with only a few fallen trees across it, knobbly underfoot due to tree roots

## Getting there

**Car:** From Hobart take the Southern Outlet (A6). Turn right into Ranelagh/Judbury Rd (C619). At Ranelagh take a right turn into North Huon Rd to Judbury. From Judbury take the Russell River Rd (also known as Lonnavale Rd), crossing the Russell River after about 5 kilometres. Keep left to Denison Rd and at crossroads go straight ahead into McDougalls Rd and go to its end (following signage to Lake Skinner Walking Track)

## Walk directions

**1** From the end of the road go straight ahead to find the entry to the track. It is marked with orange/pink ribbons and initially leads through a wet area of regrowth mixed forest with cutting grass, cheeseberry and Tasmanian pepperberry in the understorey and rainforest trees such as myrtle, leatherwood, sassafras and celery top pine joining the eucalypts in the canopy. Tree trunks are often festooned with the beautiful red-flowering climbing heath.

**2** The track begins to rise after you have passed the wet spot and you will find yourself walking through a virtual forest of very tall, endemic heath plants. Named 'pandani', this is the world's largest heath plant. You may hear the distinctive call of the mountain jay or currawong from the treetops above.

**3** The flexibility of your joints will be tested as you climb over a few fallen logs across the track. The light here always appears very green and everything seems to be covered in moss. The track becomes steeper and as you climb higher, the bush opens up and becomes less mossy. In a wet, rocky section, bauera, tea-tree and a dainty shrub and cousin

### Tasmanian flora – Tasmanian climbing heath (*Prionotes cerinthoides*)

Another Tasmanian endemic, this member of the heath family can grow from the ground or as an epiphytic on tree trunks in rainforests up to ten metres high. Its flowers are pendulous and tubular and only about two centimetres long. Flowering over a long period of time they can be found from November to April.

of the leatherwood tree (*Eucryphia milliganii*) line the track. In late spring and early summer the Tasmanian waratah puts on a fine display in this area.

**4** When you reach the top of the hill you will get your first glimpse of the Snowy Range looking across the valley created by a tributary to the Falls Rivulet, which flows out of Lake Skinner. You must traverse this valley before you veer left to go up alongside the Falls Rivulet to the lake's shore. The valley floor is strewn with very large dolerite boulders that have been transported and then dumped here by glaciers during the last ice age. The flora is rich and varied and attracts many birds, especially honeyeaters.

**5** Going up the other side of the valley you gain views back down to Lonnavale while up ahead Mount Snowy South looms larger and you can make out its distinctive dolerite columns. The vegetation is alpine here. A lot of dead trees are the legacy of bush fires.

**6** You will reach a large boulder which has an overhang and a low rock wall built around it to form a sheltered area in case you encounter some bad weather. The lake is perched just behind this boulder. King Billy pines grow on its shores. More Tasmanian waratahs can be found if you wander left along the top of the lake's rim. You can take some time for a bit of exploration and a snack before returning to the start.

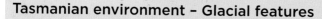

## Tasmanian environment – Glacial features

Lake Skinner fills the bottom of a cirque (large depression) which was gouged out by a glacier during a recent (geologically speaking) ice age. The gouged out boulders and rubble were pushed by the glacier as it crept down the valley and when it melted, the rocks and rubble were dropped to leave behind a dam-like structure known as a moraine. Nature's way to create a waterhole or lake – no bulldozers needed!

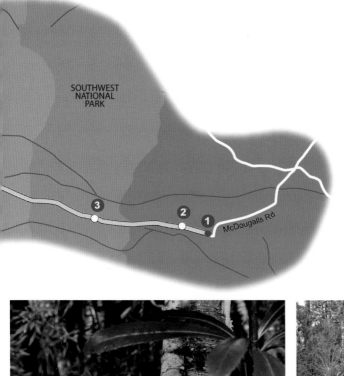

SOUTHWEST
NATIONAL
PARK

McDougalls Rd

Pandani

## Tasmanian flora – Tasmanian waratah (*Telopea truncata*)

This Tasmanian endemic shrub is commonly about three metres tall with bright red flowers that are somewhat daintier than its mainland cousin's. These plants prefer wet sclerophyll forest or subalpine scrubland at altitudes from 600 to 1200 metres. The best time to see them flowering is in November and December.

# 36 Garden Island Bay Coastal Walk

Randalls Bay and Mickey Beach are the largest and most popular beaches in the Huon area. They lie between Cray Point to the east and Echo Sugarloaf to the west in the sheltered Garden Island Bay along the Huon River Estuary. The waters here are shallow and the beaches make for safe swimming. This walk connects the two beaches, crossing a small headland with a minor detour to the point for spectacular coastal views. Extensive deposits of river gravels and sand lie inland, a legacy of different sea levels during past Ice Ages and interglacial periods. These gravels were quarried extensively until 1997 when it was recognised that they support plant communities of high conservation value such as the rare coastal species of silver peppermint. The site was declared a conservation area to protect important natural and cultural heritage values within.

## At a glance

**Grade:** Easy

**Time:** 1 hr 45 mins

**Distance:** 4.5 km return

**Ascent/Descent:** 20 m/20 m

**Conditions:** Well-made coastal track, some sections close to cliff tops, beaches; mostly sheltered

**Further information:** www.scat.org.au

### Getting there

**Car:** From Hobart take the Southern Outlet and follow signage towards Huonville (A6). At Huonville (just before the bridge) turn left into the Channel Hwy (B68). Pass through Cygnet and after about 11.5 kilometres turn right into Randalls Bay Rd and drive 2.2 kilometres to picnic shelter at Randalls Bay

## Walk directions

**1** Go down to the beach and turn right to walk towards the colourful Triassic sandstone cliffs. An old, eroded tramway, now in danger from coastal erosion, once led along their base to a jetty which was used to load local produce onto boats. The remains can be inspected with care before you begin your walk.

**2** Look to the right of a *Randalls Bay Conservation Area, Mickeys Beach 1 hr rtn* sign for a set of sandstone steps which zigzag up to the headland above the cliffs. Climb the steps then follow the gravelled path along the cliff top until you reach a Y-junction.

**3** Keep left to follow the cliff top on a narrower track which loops around the point of the headland. To the left, across Randalls Bay you can see Echo Sugarloaf in the foreground. The track returns to the main path under a canopy of tall melaleucas with views along the coast to Mickeys Beach. Try to keep to the main track here, as a lot of side tracks have been

Acacia suaveolens

created. This problem is being addressed by a dedicated Coast Care Group who hope to install some directional signs in the future to prevent further degradation.

**4** As you return to the main track you will note a high diversity of plant species along the way, including white kunzea, the small, straggly sweet-scented wattle, particularly brightly coloured trigger plants, a number of orchids and currant bush, a

many-branched shrub that appears leafless because its leaves are reduced to mere scales along the stems. It smells strongly of honey, so you are more likely to smell it before you see it.

**5** Continue along the main track which leads through beautifully restored bushland with only minor quarrying scars visible. Sunshine wattle, bull oak and its shrubby cousin, necklace she oak, native cherry and banksias are among the many plant species growing here. The birdlife in this area is equally diverse and you can expect to see honeyeaters, robins, wrens and whistlers. If you are fortunate you may be able to spot eagles above as both the sea eagle and the wedge-tailed eagle breed nearby on Garden Island.

# 36 Garden Island Bay Coastal Walk

**6** After a couple of minor crests, one of a number of shacks and houses that line the coast becomes visible through the trees on the right. The track narrows and you will note some small eucalypts with very silvery leaves. These are the rare coastal silver peppermints.

**7** Shortly you will reach an interpretive sign about flora and fauna of this area and the work of the Friends of Randalls Bay Group. A little further along some wooden steps take you down to the peaceful little Mickeys Beach which also has some impressive sandstone cliffs at its far end.

**8** Leave the beach via an obvious track that leads up the bank through the bush to a small, disused car park. Walk along the car park and up a small rise leaving a private

## Tasmanian flora – Silver peppermint (*Eucalyptus tenuiramis*)

This dainty gum tree, with its distinctive silvery (glaucous) stems and leaves, belongs to the peppermint group of eucalypts, as its common name suggests. It is a very close relative to the Tasmanian endemic risdon peppermint (*Eucalyptus risdonii*). There are a few forms of silver peppermint in Tasmania, with those growing on the west coast being quite different to the east coast variety. The variation occurs due to differences in climate and soil. In eastern Tasmania they are found growing on Permian mudstone and are relatively uncommon. The vegetation community that contains the coastal variety of *Eucalyptus tenuiramis* in the Randalls Bay Conservation Area has been declared as threatened.

property on your right. Ignore side tracks to the right as the track crosses the small headland with some wide views showing Garden Island sitting in the Bay.

**9** The track turns into a taped route and a fish farm can be seen offshore. You may come across a blue-tongue lizard, or near dusk an eastern barred bandicoot in this area. After passing a couple more private properties you will notice a steep, bricked track leading down to a small rocky bay. A large log juts into the water to serve as a jetty/swimming access platform. Take a small break in this beautiful area before retracing your steps to Randalls Bay and the start point.

## Tasmanian fauna – Blotched blue-tongue lizard

These are the largest lizards you can find in Tasmania. They grow to about 30 centimetres in length, without the tail, which is only about twelve centimetres long. When you come across them in the bush they can give you quite a fright as initially they look like a snake – until you see their short legs! They will tend to keep still when you first encounter them and will often even let you pat them. But as soon as you look away for a second they will scurry off at great speed! Blue-tongue lizards are omnivorous which means they enjoy a fancy and healthy diet of insects, snails, fungi, flowers and fruit. They are particularly partial to strawberries and will also partake in dog and cat food. Presumably due to this healthy diet they have a long life, with twenty years having been recorded. Alas, they are prone to having accidents involving lawn mowers, farm machinery, cars and snail bait. They give birth to one to fifteen live young about every other year.

# 37 Duckhole Lake

This is a leisurely, near level walk, suitable for families with younger children. It follows the route of an old timber tramway along which logs were transported, using horses, to the Strathblane mill. You may be lucky to hear or even see lyrebirds, which inhabit this area, along the way. The destination is a large, flooded sinkhole in Precambrian dolomite limestone which is part of the surrounding Karst system.

## At a glance

**Grade:** Easy

**Time:** 1 hr 30 mins

**Distance:** 4.3 km return

**Ascent/Descent:** 40 m/40 m

**Conditions:** Well-built track with long sections of duckboarding; sheltered and shady

**Further information:** www.discovertasmania.com

## Getting there

**Car:** From Hobart take the Southern Outlet (A6). Pass through Huonville, Geeveston, Dover and Strathblane. 2 kilometres south of Strathblane turn right into the Old Hastings Road. After 1.2 kilometres turn right into Darcy Link Road. After 3.5 kilometres turn left into Creekton Road. After 3 kilometres park in small car park just before bridge over Creekton Rivulet

# 37 Duckhole Lake

## Walk directions

**1** The entrance to the walking track is on your right, just before the bridge, marked by a distinctive *Great Short Walks* sign. It initially leads along the fern-lined Creekton Rivulet which has the typically tea-coloured waters you find in much of the Tasmanian wilderness. The stain is caused by tannins from plants such as buttongrass. Above, a canopy of tall eucalypts provides shade and shelter.

**2** With the creek remaining visible on your left, the track rises slightly above the creek bank. On your right is a regrowth stringybark forest which has been logged previously.

**3** Shortly the track dips down to cross a small watercourse, then follows it through a stand of manferns. You may notice a heavy cast-iron object, reminiscent of a lid from a 44-gallon drum, propped up against a tree on the left side of the track. This was used as a 'shoe' which carried the front end of a log to prevent it from sinking into the forest floor while it was pulled along by horses. Directly you will pass a stump with a very large circumference which is all that's left of the forest giant that would have been harvested using axes and handsaws.

**4** The track crosses another small watercourse which comes in from the right. From here on to the lake much of the track is duckboarded. Lyrebirds can often be found in this are and their scratching can be seen in the bush. The trees with the light grey bark and toothed, dark green leaves lining the track are sassafras. Their finely textured, pale wood with often interesting 'black heart' markings is used in crafts and furniture making. You pass a small swamp on your right and then cross a creek via a wooden bridge before continuing along a swampy area.

**5** The track soon passes between two large eucalypts, part of a stand in this area. A few steps up and with the creek to your right you cross some more minor watercourses. Cutting grass grows in the wet areas to the left side of the track.

**6** After bridging Creekton Rivulet, you will pass through an area of tea-tree with the dainty coral fern growing beneath and a small,

# 37 Duckhole Lake

circular clearing through the tall shrubs on the left. Some rainforest species endemic to Tasmania such as celery top pine, native laurel and leatherwood begin to appear. In late summer some are festooned with the beautiful small, pendulous red flowers of the Tasmanian endemic climbing heath.

**7** The duckboarding ends just a few metres before the lake and a wooden bridge that leads you across the outlet. A picnic table on your left overlooks the deep and still waters of the lake. On a clear day you will be able to see Adamsons Peak above the forest. Perhaps it is time for a snack and a rest before you retrace your steps to the start point.

## Tasmanian environment – Karst

The very ancient dolomite limestone (Precambrian – over 500 million years old) in this area contains calcium, magnesium and carbonates derived from sea shells and was originally formed through chemical processes. Compared to other rock types it is quite soft and more water soluble. Sinkholes, such as Duckhole Lake, form where surface water percolates into underground streams. The leaching action of the water gradually deepens the underground streams producing caves and caverns. Sometimes the ground above these can collapse to form new sinkholes. A landscape which displays these features was first studied in Yugoslavia on the Kras Plateau along the Adriatic Sea. The word 'karst' is derived from the German word for this region; the Italians call it carso based on a pre-Indo-European word *karra* which means 'stony'. The typical grooved features often seen in limestone are known as karren.

# 38 Southport Lagoon

Begin this lovely walk with a ride on Tasmania's last operating and Australia's southernmost bush tramway which leaves Ida Bay for Deep Hole three to four times daily. From Deep Hole it is an easy walk through open bushland to the shallow waters of Southport Lagoon.

## At a glance

**Grade:** Easy

**Time:** 2 hrs

**Distance:** 6.6 km part circuit

**Ascent/Descent:** 20 m/20 m

**Conditions:** Old vehicular track with some short, wet, muddy sections. Partly shady. It is important to check with Ida Bay Railways regarding departure times as their timetable varies according to season. However they are flexible and accommodating, particularly for larger groups

**Further information:** Ida Bay Railway, T (03) 6298 3110, Mob 0428 383 262, idabayrailway.com.au

**Getting there**

**Car:** From Hobart take the Huon Highway (A6). Turn right into C636 before Southport. Keep left at the turn-off to Hastings (about 101 kilometres from Hobart). Park in front of Ida Bay Heritage Railway station. Take the quaint little train to Deephole Bay

## Walk directions

**1** After alighting from the train onto the railway platform turn south-east towards an old Landrover wreck. Here you will find the signed entry to the sandy track which initially leads through bushland with a canopy of mixed eucalypts, blackwoods and many banksias. Parrots and honeyeaters are attracted to the rich flora in this area and can be seen and heard above.

**2** You next cross a low lying area covered in buttongrass and tea-tree, indicating that it can get quite wet underfoot.

**3** The track rises gently into very lightly timbered bush allowing lovely views back to Deep Bay. Coral fern lines some sections of the track as you walk up along the contour of a low hill on your right, moving away from the bay in a southerly direction and crossing the hill at a low saddle with an altitude of some 28 metres.

**4** Head down to cross another wet spot with melaleuca, tea-tree and buttongrass, then back into the dappled shade of light bush with casuarinas, saggs and large patches of prickly beauty with its yellow pea flowers in spring.

**5** You will cross a third buttongrass patch with a scattering of needlebush before you reach a track junction where the track to Southport Bluff turns off to the left. Keep right towards Southport Lagoon. You are now heading in a westerly direction, passing a tract of tall melaleuca shrubs that grow in a swampy area.

# 38 Southport Lagoon

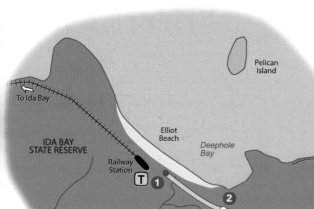

which now gradually curves north-west through very light bush with few tall trees and a heathy understorey. You may notice a small stand of silver peppermint before you reach the junction you passed earlier on your way

**6** It is not long before you emerge at the beautiful crescent-shaped beach that lines the shallow Southport lagoon. Due west you can see the impressive skyline of the Southern Mountains with the prominent peaks of Moonlight Ridge and Cockscomb. A number of shore birds can be observed here fishing in the shallow waters of the lagoon. Sea eagles can also be spotted. Go left along the beach until you see a small stick with pink flagging tape which marks your return loop.

**7** The taped route leads into thick bush and onto a faint disused vehicle track which leads up the dune and to a track junction. Keep left through a patch of melaleuca, buttongrass and bracken

fern. The track gradually rises, curving right then left. Looking back you gain lovely views across the lagoon and the mountains to its west. In spring you may see the beautiful white flag iris flowering in this area (see box on page 205).).

**8** Next you will reach a T-junction with the Southport Bluff Track. Go left along the track

to the lagoon and the end of the loop you have just walked.

**9** Go right to retrace your steps to the railway platform to catch the train back to Ida Bay.

### Tasmanian flora – White flag iris (*Diplarrena moraea*)

This pretty plant is often camouflaged because it likes to grow among saggs and tussocks. Its long, leathery leaves, growing from a basal tuft, look very similar to sagg – the only difference is that they are pointy at the tip rather than ragged. In spring and early summer, however, they put on a beautiful display when their white three-petalled flowers, borne on tall stalks, give the appearance of a swarm of white butterflies hovering over the saggs.

### Out and about – Ida Bay Railway at Lune River

The narrow gauge line (only two feet, or 610 mm) was constructed in 1922 to carry limestone from the Ida Bay quarries to Lune River Estuary and later, after this silted up, to Deep Hole Bay. The limestone was loaded onto ships and transported to Electrona on the D'Entrecastreaux Channel, where it was used in the production of calcium carbide to produce acetylene which, in combination with oxygen, is used to heat and cut steel.

The under-frames of the little, open passenger carriages you find there nowadays date back to the 1890s when they were open ore wagons. The tops were added in the 1970s. The carriages are powered by 1940s ex-army Malcolm Moore locomotives. The line has been shortened to just 6.8 km with a turning circle at Deep Bay and has become a popular holiday destination for families and tourists.

# 39 Fishers Point

A very pleasant and easy coastal stroll, with wide views of the Southern Mountains for most of the way, leads to the ruins of an historic brick cottage which was home to a maritime pilot during the mid-1800s. His job was to assist ships with navigation in the area. Nearby you can also inspect a navigation light. Parks passes apply.

## At a glance

**Grade:** Easy

**Time:** 2 hrs 15 mins

**Distance:** 7 km return

**Conditions:** Beach and rocky coast; short section of forest

**Further information:** www.parks.tas.gov.au

**Getting there**

**Car:** From Hobart take the Huon Highway (A6). Turn right into C636 before Southport. Keep left at the turn-off to Hastings (about 101 kilometres from Hobart). Follow the road south past Ida Bay. Lune River Rd becomes South Cape Rd and then becomes Cockle Creek Rd. Pass Cockle Creek, cross bridge over the Cockle Creek and continue past Ranger Station and a number of campsites to end of road to park your car in designated area

## Walk directions

**1** The walking track begins at the end of the turning circle. Walk between the boulders that have been placed there to stop cars and continue on the wide bitumen track which is lined with tall blue gums, banksias and tea-tree. Only a few steps along you will find a sign pointing toward the Whale Sculpture to the left and Fishers Point to the right.

**2** You can inspect the Whale Sculpture, a bronze by Tasmania's prolific sculptor, Stephen Walker, which is placed on a platform here. A number of informative interpretation panels tell you about the scientific work of Bruni D'Entrecasteaux's team, who came here with two frigates in search of the missing explorer La Perouse. The story of the whaling industry which took place here in Recherche Bay is told and the names of the mountains of the spectacular Southern Ranges, which you will be able to see during your

walk, are shown. You will also find some information on other tracks in the area.

**3** When you have informed yourself, return to the track junction and set off for Fishers Point. The track follows the top of the rocky shore to a small beach where some interesting shells can often be found. Walk to the far end of the beach. Wooden poles with yellow triangles mark the track and by following them, rather than the shoreline, you will keep your feet dry at high tide.

**4** You will soon reach a second beach sprinkled with rocky outcrops and a larger dolerite platform at its far end, known as Snake Point. This sloping rock slab was used by whalers to hold whale carcasses

once they were winched from the sea so that they could be skinned and the blubber removed. You may be able to find pieces of brick and other evidence of this shore-based whaling station which was established in 1835. To continue, walk through some small grassy areas to the next, larger beach. The beaches are lined with a backdrop of tall, dense bush dominated by blue gums, wattles and tea-tree with an understorey of bracken and reeds.

**5** About two thirds along this beach you will note a wooden rail at the top of the bank. A short climb will reveal an old gravestone, that of Samuel Thomas Pryat who died on board of the whaler Aladdin. Continue along the beach and skirt around a rocky section (that may become a little inundated at high tide), towards the point ahead, which bears another wooden marker. A fourth beach is reached after you pass this marker.

**6** The track turns inland at the next marker to cross the 'tongue' of Fishers Point. This short bush section leads through tall, shady vegetation. It emerges at a more exposed shore strewn with boulders where you will shortly reach a sign pointing to *Ruins* on the right and *Lighthouse* to the left.

**7** Take the track to the ruins: it can be a bit overgrown with bracken at times, but as the brick structure is clearly visible through the bush, it will not be hard to find. Another interpretation panel to follow up on the whaling story and the piloting days has been installed here. Although the cottage was only small it was very strongly built with four thicknesses of bricks. During summer and autumn you may notice some fuchsia flowers among the ruins. While they are very pretty, they are one of the many 'garden escapes' that can be found in the Tasmanian bush. Some of these such

as foxgloves and Spanish heath (*Erica lusitanica*, see walk 31) have become very invasive. Many volunteer groups assist the Parks and Wildlife Service and other environmental organisations to control garden escapes and weeds.

**8** From the ruin you can take a shortcut through the bracken to reach the eastern shore which here carries a lot of shellgrit. A left turn will lead you to the navigation light and you can continue to round the point here to begin your return walk. You will get a superior view of the Southern Ranges on your way back; you will also be able to see Cockle Creek from this direction.

## Tasmanian history – Samuel Thomas Pryat

Whaling was an important industry during early settlement of Tasmania. During its peak of production in the mid to late 1830s whale oil and bone was the second largest export item from Tasmania after wool and the industry was a significant source of employment. But the work was hard and dangerous and took its toll. The untimely death of Samuel Thomas Pryat at only 29 years of age, on board the whaler Aladdin when it was at Tasmania's Southwest Cape, illustrates this. It is thought that Tasmania's last full-blooded Aboriginal man William Lanney (also known as King Billy) was a shipmate to Pryat. King Billy was born in 1835 and began work on the wharves in Hobart, then went on to whaling and was a particularly skilful lancer. He became ill with choleric diarrhoea after a whaling trip and also died at only 34 years of age.

The inscription on Pryat's grave reads:
*Sacred to*
*the memory of*
*Samuel Thomas Pryat*
*who died on the 9th of April 18 (unreadable)*
*on board of the Aladdin whaler off SW Cape*
*aged 29 years*
*In the midst of life we are in death*

# 40 Montrose to MONA

The first stage of a new foreshore walk, which includes an interesting boardwalk across the shallow waters' edge of Elwick Bay, has been completed recently by the Glenorchy City Council. This walk leads through the very popular Montrose Foreshore Community Park with one of Hobart's best children's playgrounds. You can combine it with a visit to the recently opened (Jan 2011) and internationally acclaimed MONA (Museum of Old and New Art), created by Glenorchy born, professional gambling millionaire David Walsh. Walsh brutally challenges visitors' ideas and beliefs on subjects such as art, religion, sex and death. The museum is situated on the beautiful Moorilla Estate on the Berriedale peninsula with its sandstone cliffs and includes a winery and restaurant. While this walk is suitable for children, only parents can decide whether entry to the museum will benefit them.

## At a glance

**Grade:** Medium

**Time:** Allow 3 hrs plus extra for museum visit

**Distance:** 8.2 km return

**Conditions:** Boardwalk, footpaths, highway overpass and a couple of road crossings; mostly exposed. Entry to MONA is free for Tasmanian residents, otherwise $20 adults, $15 concession, opening hours 1000–1700 (last admission 1630), closed on Tuesdays

**Further information:** www.gcc.tas.gov.au, mona.net.au, Mona reception T (03) 6277 9900

**Getting there**

**Car:** Drive to the Derwent Entertainment Centre (DEC) situated on the Brooker Highway in Glenorchy, south of Hobart and park in the large car park nearest to the building

## Walk directions

**1** Walk towards the foreshore where you will reach a concrete path.

**2** The track leads onto a colourful boardwalk across the inlet of Barossa Creek and a small wetland, then passes a *GASP* sign (Glenorchy Art & Sculpture Park).

**3** To your left you can see the small sculpture park with the City of Glenorchy and the Welllington Range forming an impressive backdrop.

**4** Ducks, gulls and native hens go about their business seemingly unperturbed by the traffic around them in this area. A large new picnic shelter with two electric barbecues is a little further along where a sign also gives directions to MONA and Montrose, back to DEC and to Wilkinsons Point (earmarked for development in 2012/13).

**5** The boardwalk continues parallel to the Brooker Highway and then along Elwick Bay to the Montrose Foreshore Community Park via a shared concrete pathway.

**6** After passing four strategically placed picnic shelters, a small outdoor gym and two barbecue shelters you will reach a car park, toilets and a large playground.

## Tasmanian history – Moorilla Estate

The Italian born immigrant turned industrialist Claudio Alcorso established the very successful Silk and Textiles business in Tasmania in 1947. He employed up to 1400 people in spinning, weaving and printing raw silk and in the production of cotton furnishings and sheets. Immigrant workers were involved in the running of the factory and shared its profits. The business eventually became part of Sheridan and was moved to mainland Australia. However the Alcorso family had made its home on the Berriedale Peninsula. In 1958 Claudio Alcorso founded the Moorilla Estate vineyard on the peninsula by planting Riesling vines. He is credited with pioneering the Tasmanian winemaking industry. Alcorso was also a keen patron of the arts and an environmentalist, actively protesting against the damming of the Franklin River in 1982.

**7** Continue along the foreshore path which leads past the Glenorchy Rowing Club building, Montrose Bay Yacht Club jetty and several boat ramps. Looking northwards across the bay you can see the white silos belonging to Cadbury Chocolate Factory, and looking east, Mount Direction.

**8** When you reach the back entrance to Montrose Bay (formerly Rosetta) High School, turn left to walk back towards the Brooker Highway between the school's main building and their playing fields and netball courts. Cross the highway using the overpass and go right to continue along the footpath to the corner of Brooker Highway and Dodson Street.

**9** Turn left into Dodson Street, pass Stourton Street and locate the entry to the shared footpath/cycleway before a right-hand turn in Dodson Street. Carefully cross the railway line (this single line is the only railway connection to the north of the state).

**10** Go right and follow the track which runs next to the railway line, separated by a tall fence. An underpass under the old Main Road is 'decorated' with the usual layers of graffiti which you

may find interesting or hate according to your outlook. There is a tiny playground with a picnic shelter and another underpass, this time under the Brooker Highway, also

colourfully lined with graffiti. Shortly you will reach an intersection with Berriedale Road. An old wooden Tasmanian Government Railways cottage stands just before the intersection. It was built around 1910 and is now in private hands.

**11** Carefully cross Berriedale Road and walk by the International Peace Forest and another

small playground on the left with the back of the Granada Tavern on the right. After passing this, looking across the road, you will be able to see the understated entrance

to MONA, the vineyard behind it and the museum perched on a hill above.

**12** Follow the track as it gently curves to the right until you reach

Alcorso Dr

Cameron Bay

Chardonnay Dr

Main Rd

12  13

14

BERRIEDALE

MONA Gallery

Berriedale Bay

Berriedale Rd

11

Brooker Hwy

Driscoll St

Main Rd

Parramore St

ROSETTA

Glenmore St

Riverview Pde

Lorraine Cr

9

10

Marys Hope Rd

Main Rd

an exit from the footpath/cycleway to safely cross the Main Road.

**13** Go up, back to the MONA entry gate and walk uphill to the museum and restaurant complex, where perhaps you can enjoy a well-earned rest and a glass of wine, visit the museum or just explore the area.

**14** For your return walk turn left from the exit gate of MONA, walk along the footpath of Main Road, carefully cross at the next traffic island, turn right into Berriedale Road then left back into the footpath/cycleway retracing your steps from here. You also have the option of following the footpath of Main Road all the way to the Brooker Highway then along the highway until you reach the High School and retrace your steps from there. This route is slightly shorter but

has a very narrow footpath section with much vehicular traffic whizzing by.

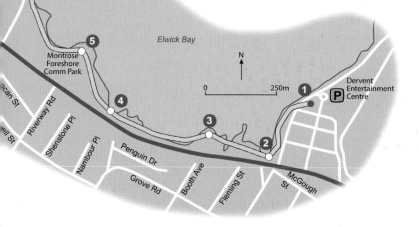

MONA entrance to museum

# Plant name glossary

Please note that plants sometimes have more than one common name, and spellings can differ. Below you can find the botanical names for all the plants mentioned in this guide.

| Common name | Scientific name |
| --- | --- |
| banksia | *Banksia marginata* |
| berry bush | *Cyathodes* |
| black peppermint/peppermint gum | *Eucalyptus amygdalina* |
| black wattle | *Acacia mearnsii* |
| black-eyed Susan | *Tetratheca pilosa* |
| blackwood | *Acacia melanoxylon* |
| blanket bush/leaf | *Bedfordia* |
| blue gum | *Eucalyptus globulus* |
| blue love creeper | *Comesperma volubile* |
| bluebell | *Wahlenbergia* |
| boobyalla/coastal wattle | *Acacia sophorae* |
| bull oak | *Allocasuarina littoralis* |
| buttongrass | *Gymnoschoenus sphaerocephalus* |
| celery top pine | *Phyllocladus aspleniifolius* |
| cheeseberry | *Cyathodes glauca* |

Cheeseberry

Mountain Pepper

Native Cranberry

| common heath | *Epacris impressa* |
| coral fern | *Gleichenia dicarpa* |
| currant bush | *Leptomeria drupacea* |
| cutting grass | *Gahnia grandis* |
| daisy bush | *Olearia phlogopappa* |
| dogwood | *Pomaderris apetala* |
| dolly bush | *Cassinia aculeata* |
| dragon heath | *Richea dracophylla* |
| fishbone fern | *Blechnum nudum* |
| fringe myrtle | *Calytrix tetragona* |
| grass tree | *Xanthorroea australis* |
| guinea flower | *Hibbertia procumbens* |
| guitar plant | *Lomatia tinctoria* |
| hakea | *Hakea microcarpa* |
| heath myrtle | *Thryptomene micrantha* |
| King Billy pine | *Athrotaxis selaginoides* |
| leatherwood | *Eucryphia lucida* |
| manuka/tea-tree | *Leptospermum scoparium* |
| mountain correa | *Correa lawrenciana* |
| myrtle | *Nothofagus cunninghamii* |
| narrow-leafed wattle | *Acacia mucronata* |
| native cherry/wild cherry | *Exocarpos cupressiformis* |
| native currant | *Coprosma quadrifida* |
| native daphne | *Pultanaea daphnoides* |

# Plant name glossary

| | |
|---|---|
| native dog rose/Bauera | *Bauera rubioides* |
| native fuchsia/wild fuschia | *Correa reflexa* |
| native hop bush | *Dodonaea viscosa* |
| native laurel | *Anopterus glandulosa* |
| necklace she-oak | *Allocasuarina monilifera* |
| needlebush | *Hakea lissosperma* |
| Norfolk Island pine | *Araucaria heterophylla* |
| Oyster Bay pine | *Callitris rhomboidea* |
| pandani | *Richea pandanifolia* |
| pink berry | *Cyathodes juniperina* |
| prickly beauty | *Pultanaea juniperina* |
| prickly box | *Bursaria spinosa* |
| prickly mimosa | *Acacia verticillata* |
| rice flower | *Pimelia nivea* |
| rosy baeckea | *Baeckea ramosissima* |
| running postman | *Kennedia prostrata* |
| sagg | *Lomandra longifolia* |
| sassafras | *Atherosperma moschatum* |
| scented paperbark | *Melaleuca squarrosa* |
| she-oak | *Allocasuarina verticillata* |
| shrubby native olive | *Notalia ligustrina* |
| silver peppermint | *Eucalyptus tenuiramis* |
| silver wattle | *Acacia dealbata* |

White Flag Iris

Parrot Pea

Melaleuca

| slender speedwell | *Veronica gracilis* |
|---|---|
| stinkwood | *Zierea arborescens* |
| stringybark | *Eucalyptus delegatensis* |
| sunshine wattle | *Acacia terminalis* |
| sweet-scented wattle | *Acacia suaveolens* |
| Tasmanian blanket bush/leaf | *Bedfordia linearis* |
| Tasmanian climbing heath | *Prionotes cerinthoides* |
| Tasmanian flax lily | *Dianella tasmanica* |
| Tasmanian pepperberry/mountain pepper | *Tasmannia lanceolata* |
| Tasmanian speedwell | *Veronica formosa* |
| Tasmanian waratah | *Telopea truncata* |
| tree fern | *Dicksonia antarctica* |
| trigger plant | *Stylidium graminifolium* |
| white correa | *Correa alba* |
| white flowering candles | *Stackhousia monogyna* |
| white gum | *Eucalyptus viminalis* |
| white kunzea | *Kunzea ambigua* |
| woolly tea-tree | *Leptospermum lanigerum* |
| yellow bottlebrush | *Callistemon pallidus* |
| yellow hakea | *Hakea nodosa* |

# Index

## A-B

Aboriginal history
    Coles Bay, 19
Amos, Margaret, 26
Archer, John Lee, 151
Australian Three Peaks Race, 19
Bark Mill Museum, 67
Barossa Creek, 211
Bernacchis Creek, 45, 55, 59
Big River Tribe, 147
black currawong, 45
blotched blue-tongue lizard, 197
bluestone, 33
Bluestone Bay, 32
Bream Creek, 95
Browns Caves, 177
Browns Caves Creek, 175
brush-tailed possum, 189
burls, 185
bushwalking clubs, 7
button grass, 29

## C

Callington Flour Mill, 141
Camp Falls, 103
Cape Barren goose, 63
Cape Tourville, 31
Casaveen Knitwear factory, 138
cattle, 146
Caves Track, 175
Chauncy, Nan, 177
cheeseberry, 89
children, walking with, 5
Clyde River, 145
Coal Mine Hill, 127
Coal Mines Historic Site, 127
Coal River, 151
Coal River Historical Society, 150
Cole, Silas, 19

Coles Bay, 17
Commandant's Cottage, 132
Counsel Creek, 49
Creekton Rivulet, 199
Crescent Bay, 115
cutting grass, 122
Cygnet River, 159

## D-E

Dead Island, 79
Deep Hole Bay, 205
Denison Canal, 95
dogs, walking with, 5
dogwood, 62
dolertie, 168
Duck Park, 69
dunes, 37
echidna, 109
Engine House, 56
Engineer's House, 61
environment, 6

## F-G

Falls Rivulet, 192
first aid, 7
Fisheries Creek, 21
Fishers Point, 207
Flat Rock Reserve, 175
Forest Track, 88
forty-spotted pardalote, 47
Fossil Cliff Circuit, 56
Freshwater Lagoon, 35
glacial features, 192
granite, 29

## H-I

Hazard, Captain Albert 'Black', 25
Hazards Beach, 23, 24
Hidden Falls, 184

Hopground Beach, 51
Hudson Cottage, 134
Hunt, Mrs Ruby, 52
Ida Bay Railway, 205
International Peace Forest, 212

## J-L

Jack jumpers, 8
Judds Creek, 187
karst, 201
Lagoon Beach, 117
Lake Dulverton, 138
*Leptospermum grandiflorum*, 164
Lisdillon, 74
Little Bluestone, 32
Long Spit, 96
Loontitetermairrelehoiner track, 68
Lost Falls Creek, 163
Lune River, 205
Luther Point, 83

## M-N

Maingon Blowhole, 113
manfern, 161
Maria Island
    Engine House, 56
    forty-spotted pardalote, 47
    history, 41-43
    Oast House, 53
    permian rocks, 57
Meredith, Charles, 71
Meredith, George, 71
Mickeys Beach, 195
Miller's Cottage, 57
Montrose Foreshore Community
    Park, 211
Moorilla Estate, 211
Mount Amos, 21, 27

Mount Clark, 122
Mount Mayson, 24
Mount Stewart, 125
mountain jay, 45
mountain pepper, 88
Muirs Beach, 18
musk, 123
navigation, 9
Nelson Creek, 167

## O-P

Oak Lodge, 150
Old Ross Burial Ground, 133
olive whistler, 188
Orford quarries, 85
Oyster Bay pine, 85
Painted Cliffs, 49
Permian rocks, 57
Plas Newyd, 70
Plummers Creek, 122
Plunkett Point, 126
Portuguese heath, 173
Pryat, Samuel Thomas, 209
public transport, 2

## Q-R

Quakers, 75
Queens Park, 145
Randalls Bay, 195
Remarkable Cave, 113
Reservoir Circuit, 55
Richardsons Beach, 17
Richmond Gaol, 151
River Pools, 163
Riverside Loop, 155
Robinson, George Augustus, 147
Ross Bridge, 133

# Index

## S

safety, 7
Saltwater Lagoon, 35
Sandspit River, 91
sandstone, 140
Schouten Beach, 69
Schouten House, 69
seaweed, 37
silver peppermint, 196
Skipping Ridge, 46, 61
snakes, 8
soft tree fern, 161
Southport Bluff Track, 204
Southport Lagoon, 203
Spanish heath, 173
spiny anteater, 109
Spring Bay Hotel, 77
sunshine wattle, 156

## T

Tasman Coastal Track, 102
Tasman Monument, 97
Tasmania climbing heath, 191
Tasmanian agriculture
  cattle, 146
Tasmanian birdlife
  black currawong, 45
  Cape Barren goose
  mountain Jay, 45
  olive whistler, 188
Tasmanian environment
  bluestone, 33
  burls, 185
  button grass, 29
  dolerite, 168
  dunes, 37
  Flat Rock Reserve, 175
  glacial features, 192
  granite, 29

  karst, 201
  Oyster Bay pine, 85
  Remarkable Cave, 113
  The Totem Pole, 110
  TLC, 176
  triassic sandstone, 119
Tasmanian fauna
  blotched blue-tongue lizard, 197
  brush-tailed possum, 189
  echidna, 109
  spiny anteater, 109
  wallabies, 91
  wombat, 49
  White's skink, 169
Tasmanian flora, 216-219
  cheeseberry, 89
  cutting grass, 122
  *Leptospermum grandiflorum*, 164
  manfern, 161
  mountain pepper, 88
  musk, 123
  Portuguese heath, 173
  silver peppermint, 196
  soft tree fern, 161
  Spanish heath, 173
  sunshine wattle, 156
  Tasmanian climbing heath, 191
  Tasmanian waratah, 193
  waxlip orchid, 118
  white flag iris, 205
Tasmanian history
  Big River Tribe, 147
  Callington Flour Mill, 141
  Coal Mines Historic Site, 127
  Denison Canal, 95
  early occupation of Coles Bay, 19
  early settlers, 172
  John Lee Archer, 151
  Lisdillon, 74

Meredith family, 71

Moorilla Estate, 211

Orford quarries, 85

Pryat, Thomas Samuel, 209

Quakers, 75

Swansea, 71

Tasman Monument, 97

The Hazards, 25

*They Found a Cave,* 177

Triabunna woodchip mill, 79

Tasmanian industry
   seaweed, 37

Tasmanian waratah, 193

Tasmanian Wool Centre, 131

The Hazards, 16

The Totem Pole, 110

*They Found a Cave,* 177

TLC, 176

Triabunna woodchip mill, 79

triassic sandstone, 119

Twelve Apostles, 45, 55, 59

**W**

walk grades, 2

walk times, 3

Walker, Stephen, 207

walking with children, 5

walking with dogs, 5

wallabies, 91

Waterfall Bay, 102

Waterfall Bluff, 101

Waterloo Point, 68

waxlip orchid, 118

what to take, 4

white flag iris, 205

White's skink, 169

Wineglass Bay, 23

Wineglass Bay Lookout and Hazards
   Circuit, 21

wombat, 49

Wombat Track, 167

# Further reading

Glazik, R, Askey-Doran M & Black, L *Tasmanian Streambank Plants*, Rivercare Section, Department of Primary Industries, Water and Environment, Hobart, 2004.

Kirkpatrick, JB & Backhouse, S *An Illustrated Guide to Tasmanian Native Trees*, Mercury-Walch, Moonah, 1981.

Launceston Field Naturalists Club, *Guide to Flowers and Plants of Tasmania*, Reed, Sydney, 1981.

Leaman, D *Step into History in Tasmanian Reserves*, Leaman Geophysics, Hobart, 2001.

Leaman, D *Walk into History in Southern Tasmania*, Leaman Geophysics, Hobart, 1999.

Minchin, RF *Wildflowers of Tasmania*, Peregrine Pty Ltd, Kettering, 2005.

Scanlon, AP, Fish, GJ & Yaxley, ML *Behind the Scenery – Tasmania's Landforms and Geology*, Department of Education, Tasmania, 1990.

Simpson, K & Day, N *The Birds of Australia*, Claremont, South Yarra, 1984.

Watts, D *Tasmanian Mammals - A Field Guide*, Peregrine Press, Kettering, 1993.

Tasmanian Parks and Wildlife Service website, www.parks.tas.gov.au

# About the author

Ingrid Roberts is a keen bushwalker and photographer and has explored many wonderful Tasmanian walking tracks during the 50 years she has lived in the state. She has a background in farming and horticulture and has been a member of the Australian Plant Society, and was a founding member of the newly opened Tasmanian Bushland Garden on the East Coast which showcases the native flora of South-East Tasmania. She holds a BA (Hons) in Geography and Environmental Studies. Through this guide she hopes to inspire the reader to go walking in Eastern Tasmania, which is the best way to get to know this beautiful part of Australia's island state with its unique natural wonders and cultural heritage. As a bonus she hopes that walkers will enjoy the increased fitness and health that regular walking can offer.

# Photography

All of the photographs in this book were taken by the author with the exception of the olive whistler on page 188 which is by Peter Marmion and the photos on pages 21 and 25, courtesy of Tourism Tasmania.

# Acknowledgments

Thanks to all at Woodslane, particularly Andrew Swaffer, Veechi Stuart, Natasha Wyndham and Kate Rowe for their helpfulness. Also a special thanks to my partner Graham and members of my extended family, Steffi, Andrew, Emily, Samuel, Heather, Christopher and Emma, who variously gave their time as walk companions and assisted with research and proofreading. Thanks also to Sue Meech, Tim Ackroyd and Peter Marmion for suggesting walks and acting as walk companions and to Katrina from the Triabunna visitor centre for generously sending me details about sights in Triabunna. Finally, thank you to Coral Lee for the design of the book, and to Pablo Candia for the cartography.

# Woodslane Press

This book is just one of a growing series of outdoor guides from Australian publishers Woodslane Press and sister imprint Boiling Billy. If your local bookshop does not have stock of a Woodslane Press or Boiling Billy title, they can easily order it for you. In case of difficulty please contact our customer service team on 02 8445 2300 or info@woodslane.com.au or order directly at www.travelandoutdoor.com.au.

.Titles include:

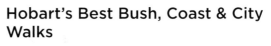

### Hobart's Best Bush, Coast & City Walks

$29.99 • ISBN: 9781921683664

### Melbourne's Best Bush, Bay & City Walks

$29.99 • ISBN: 9781921874352

### Best Walks of Geelong, the Bellarine & Brisbane Ranges

$29.99 • ISBN: 9781921874819

### Pet Friendly Accommodation on Australia's East Coast

$34.95 • ISBN: 9781921874130

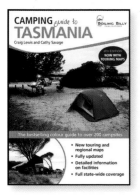

**Camping Guide to Tasmania**

$24.99

ISBN: 9781921606144

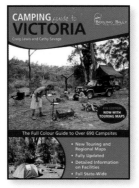

**Camping Guide to Victoria**

$29.99

ISBN: 9781921203671

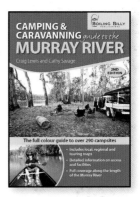

**Caravan and Camping Guide to the Murray River**

$29.99

ISBN: 9781921874970

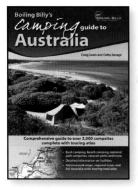

**Boiling Billy's Camping Guide to Australia**

$49.99

ISBN: 9781922131119

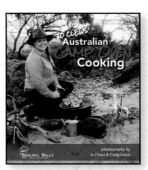

**Australian Camp Oven Cooking**

$34.99

ISBN: 9781922131003

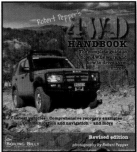

**Robert Pepper's 4WD Handbook**

$44.99

ISBN: 9781921874789

All Woodslane Press and Boiling Billy books are available for bulk and custom purposes. Volume copies of this and our other titles are available at wholesale prices, and custom-jacketed and even mini-extracts are possible. Contact our Publishing Manager for further information, on (02) 8445 2300 or info@woodslane.com.au.

# Notes

# Notes

# MAP SYMBOLS & LEGEND

| Symbol | Description | Symbol | Description |
|---|---|---|---|
| (i) | Tourist Information | ——— | Dam Wall |
| (T) | Toilet | — | Marina/Wharf/Jetty |
| (P) | Parking | | Lake/Large River |
| ☕ | Café | | River/Creek |
| 🚌 | Bus Stop | | Ferry Route |
| 🖐 | Aboriginal Site | ▭▭▭▭ | Walking Track |
| 🎨 | Public Art | - - - - - - - | Walking Track Variation |
| 🏊 | Swimming | ▮▮▮▮▮▮▮ | Board Walk |
| 🚲 | Bike/Walking Track | ▭▭▭ | Foot Bridge |
| 🚲 | Bike Track | ▨▨▨ | Stairs |
| ⛱ | Beach | - - - - - - | Fire Trail |
| 🛎 | Picnic Area | ——— | Road |
| 🪑 | Seating Bench | ▯▯▯▯▯ | Bridge |
| 🎠 | Childrens Playground | ⊢⊦━━⊦⊣ | Railway Line/Station |
| ▲ | Camping Area | ⌐⌐⌐⌐ | Escarpment/Cliff |
| ▪ | Point of Interest | ⊂◌◌◌⊃ | Rocky Shoreline |
| △ | Summit | ▭ | Beach/Sand Dunes |
| ○❶ | Place of interest | ▭ | Ocean |
| ≼ | View Point/Lookout | ▭ | Residential |
| ✚ | Hospital | | |
| 🍖 | BBQ | | |
| ⛴ | Ferry Terminal/Route | N ↑ | |
| ⊢⊣ | Locked Gate | 0 ___ 200 m   Scale | |

# Your thoughts appreciated!

We do hope that you are enjoying using this book, but we know that nothing in this world is perfect and your suggestions for improving on this edition would be much appreciated.

Your name _____

Your address or email address _____

_____

_____

Your contact phone number _____

Are you a resident or visitor to the SE Tasmania? _____

What you most liked about this book _____

_____

_____

What you least liked about this book _____

_____

_____

Which is your favourite walk featured in this book?

_____

Which walk wasn't featured but you think should have been included?

_____

Would you like us to keep you informed of other Woodslane books?
If so: are you interested in:

☐ walking                          ☐ general outdoor activities

☐ visiting natural & historic sites  ☐ activities in the SE Tasmanian region only

☐ picnicking                       ☐ activities in Tasmania

☐ cycling                          ☐ activities around Australia

What others books would you like to see in this series?

_____

_____

**Woodslane Pty Ltd • 10 Apollo St • Warriewood • NSW 2102**
**Fax: 02 9997 5850 • Email: info@woodslane.com.au**

TRAVEL WIDELY. TREAD LIGHTLY

www.kleankanteen.com.au